Dr Amy Thunig (B.Arts, M.Teach, PhD) is a Gomeroi/Gamilaroi/Kamilaroi yinarr (woman) and mother who resides on the unceded lands of the Awabakal peoples. An academic in the field of education, Amy is also a Director at Sydney Story Factory in Redfern, and in 2019 delivered their TEDx talk: 'Disruption is not a dirty word'. As well as being on various committees and councils, Amy is a media commentator and panellist, regularly appearing on television programs such as ABC's *The Drum*, and writing for publications such as *Buzzfeed*, *Sydney Review of Books*, *IndigenousX*, *The Guardian* and more.

PRAISE FOR TELL ME AGAIN

'Amy Thunig's survival amidst chaos, addiction and poverty will leave you questioning your unconscious bias. Through love, forgiveness and a will to succeed, Amy has risen against the odds to become a voice Australia needs.' – **Narelda Jacobs**

'Lyrical, moving and above all life-affirming, *Tell Me Again* is a masterful memoir.' – **Clementine Ford**

'To have gone through everything Amy has – yet survive and thrive – is one thing, but to also turn it into such a striking piece of writing? Amazing!' – **Lindsay McDougall**

'"If I was to ask you whose land you were on, you'd be able to tell me?" With just seventeen words, broadcast on prime-time television during *The Bachelorette,* Amy Thunig began a powerful, humanising and deeply present conversation between modern Australia and our knowledge of First Nations people. Her book, *Tell Me Again*, is a sharp and devastating account of a young woman growing up in the face of impenetrable systemic bias, discrimination and violence. A must-read for anyone who wishes for Australia to accept the ongoing legacy of our colonial history and move towards a better future for all of us.' – **Osher Günsberg**

TELL
A MEMOIR # ME
AGAIN
AMY
THUNIG

UQP

First published 2022 by University of Queensland Press
PO Box 6042, St Lucia, Queensland 4067 Australia

University of Queensland Press (UQP) acknowledges the Traditional Owners and their
custodianship of the lands on which UQP operates. We pay our respects to their Ancestors
and their descendants, who continue cultural and spiritual connections to Country.
We recognise their valuable contributions to Australian and global society.

uqp.com.au
reception@uqp.com.au

Cover design by Josh Durham / Design By Committee
Cover photograph by Dru Maher-Brooks / Iron Monkey Photography
Typeset in 12.5/17.5 pt Bembo Std by Post Pre-press Group, Brisbane
Printed in Australia by McPherson's Printing Group

  University of Queensland Press is assisted by the
Australian Government through the Australia
Council, its arts funding and advisory body.

A catalogue record for this book is available from the National Library of Australia.

ISBN 978 0 7022 6584 6 (pbk)
ISBN 978 0 7022 6741 3 (epdf)
ISBN 978 0 7022 6742 0 (epub)

University of Queensland Press uses papers that are natural, renewable and recyclable products
made from wood grown in well-managed forests and other controlled sources. The logging and
manufacturing processes conform to the environmental regulations of the country of origin.

I dedicate this book to my children E and K.
Of all the wonderful, delightful, incredible joys
I am blessed to experience in this life,
being your Mumma is my favourite.

PROLOGUE

W E ARE TOLD THAT A person's worth is either whole or non-existent. That our nature, that our being, is singular. But lives and hearts and characters are multifaceted, and while it would perhaps be most comforting for me to say that I only learnt what *not* to do through this home, and these parents, that would be unfair and dishonest. The same people who in clear ways failed me – who struggled with their addiction only to repeatedly succumb – also built me up and taught me the lessons and qualities that have led to my success. I am of them.

I was the worst kind of child for people with these challenges. I rarely understood when to keep quiet; I regularly did my best to sabotage the acts I disagreed with – hiding, ripping up and flushing them. I had demands – the demands of childhood and growth – and I made them of people already in a state of overwhelm. In the midst of the battles, they were bound to

1

fight through choices they did and did not make. They tried, and they tried consistently.

A note written before the sun came up: *It is better to die standing, than to live life on your knees.* I see Dad in my twelve-year-old mind's eye, as I hold the scrap of paper in my hand, marked with the rim of his coffee cup. He sat here and wrote this to me while having coffee, before packing the esky and preparing to leave for work, time looped to speak in handwriting what time wouldn't allow to be uttered.

And so, although they struggled, and we struggled as a family, my parents wrote these lessons on paper, in my heart, in my mind, and I was blessed to be born into a family and community ancient and filled with love, even amidst brokenness. There is power in story; in telling mine and ours, I hope to humanise that which is too often dehumanised, and highlight that which is too often erased. There is hope, but even without change, a person's value is inherent.

I often wonder about timelines and the way a Eurocentric view positions time as linear but as Indigenous peoples we are raised to understand time as circular. Within a circular understanding of life: time, energy and generations coexist. Coexistence with and within Country on lands, within waterways, and in skies. Our accountability and obligations are therefore to our ancestors, *and* our descendants, as well as to ourselves.

When my success as an adult is queried in the context of a difficult childhood, I think sometimes perhaps what they mean is *how did I have the audacity to dream so big* and be *so sure* that

I should pursue my goals when there was no clear roadmap provided for me, or because in their mind, *I had no right.*

I do not know the simple way of saying that child-me could see and feel future-me, that our coexistence within circular time meant we conversed and encouraged one another, and as we are one and the same, I knew where I would land even though I could not see how I would journey there. Exchanges of energy and love, across time spent in the same locations, encouraged by ancestors.

My grandfather still lives in the same house that both I and my mother were grown up and loved within. Today I go there with my own children: that's four generations of bloodlines and childhoods cycling and circling upon the same land and within the same small rooms.

As a grown woman, when I walk up the green metal stairs to my grandfather's back door, I feel the presence of my child-self playing there; I am also laying out on the soft grass under the clothesline where the magpies have for generations sat and sung. If you want that grass to be soft, you have to plan seasons ahead, adjust and intervene with what will otherwise grow there, and scout for burrs in the places you may wish for children to be able to play.

I watch my children eat from the strong, fruitful mulberry tree – climbing those same branches that I climbed and took from – that grew and bloomed before I had taken my first breath or they theirs. The energy of aunties and cousins yarning over cups of tea in the shade of that tree, echo and remain, even if the sun-bleached chairs they sat on have long since disintegrated. Together we all hear my grandfather complain about the bats leaving their purple droppings on the washing, and reflect that those bats have been ruining his washing for generations, and yet the clothesline has never been moved.

As a grown woman I am often approached for knowledge and guidance by the very people who I've overheard dehumanise my family and myself by association: those who want to erase me, my family, our lives from the storying of this world and the framing of who is deemed 'worthy'. I live within the complexity of these interweavings: in the telling of coded language in academic spaces, in the polished face presented consciously on panels and television screens, in the silence forced by decorum of polite conversations.

Lives are built of messy interactions, exchanges and experiences but complexities are rarely welcomed in 'civilised' spaces. You hear ad nauseum in the academy that every article tells a story but no article can tell every story; you must simplify, not distract, instead make it smooth, not personal. Your existence is politicised: the very people who have used terms like 'junkies' in front of you won't actually understand why you struggle with them; instead if they *know* they will write you off or label you *the exception*. There are no exceptions.

I saw a counsellor once, I told her one story, and she cried.

I told a teacher, who told the principal, and we sat with the phone on loudspeaker as community services said: *No-one wants a teenager.*

I regularly drive past the very street I walked along with no jumper in the pouring rain, determined to do better, to be better, and to take my family with me.

I sit at my desk completing a thesis: knowing the time is arriving when I will be seated on an academic stage as Dr Thunig, and future-me watches as my kin cross that same stage, attaining degrees. We are each in our regalia. Our families stand in the audience and cry – they shout and holler their joy because they don't know *that isn't what you do* in these spaces – and I for one am constantly ready to fight anyone who tries to silence them. This is Stolen Land: do not tell us how to celebrate. These spaces need our hollering and cooees: our loud Indigenous joy.

Our energy and our presence is already there and here – a future echo – waiting for us to arrive.

PART
ONE

1

'BAALUU DHURRALAANHA – THE MOON IS RISING,' I whisper to my children as we drive towards the camp site. We are journeying through Gomeroi Country to be by the water with our Old People. It is an eight-hour drive from our home on Awabakal Country and though we left not long after sun up, the moon has now become visible in the early evening sky and we are still driving. I am grateful for air conditioning and roadside stops.

'Mum?' My eldest child, head of thick dark hair, is emerging out of that sleep state that comes from the rocking of a car on a long drive.

'Mmm?'

'Tell me again about the night I was born?'

Though physically I am now with Gomeroi Country, this question sends my mind drifting back to Awabakal; to the waters and paths I moved over when labouring. The same lands and waterways my own mother moved over and with when birthing me, the same Country my father was born into.

I drive on and begin to story with my child about the journey of bringing them earthside. I reminisce on the way it began with eating juicy watermelon at their grandmother's house, and ended with ten pounds of perfection with big green eyes staring up at me from within my arms.

Like my child, I always loved to ask my mother about the night I was born, and like my mother, I do not share all the details of their birth with my child, knowing that can wait for when they are older.

Windows wound down, air streaming in to take the edge off the summer heat, we drive along the winding roads to Great-Grandma Lucy's house on Yuin Country. We are off to spend time with the woman, home and Country that shaped and nurtured your own adolescence. You bring us to your grandma's every chance you can but I am not a great traveller.

The motion of the car taking each corner along the coast churns my belly as I rest on the back seat, eyes closed as the dappled lighting makes shadows across my eyelids. We have no air conditioning, and the intense heat doesn't help the motion sickness you and I both get.

'Mum?' I sit up and lean into the space between the two front seats.

'Mmm.' In the front passenger seat, your eyes are closed against the motion sickness, head resting on the door frame.

'Tell me again about the night I was born?'

'*Again?*' You laugh but start the story again and I am ecstatic.

You always begin by telling me you were wearing Nan's nightgown; you hadn't packed enough clothing, a short stay run long. I beg for more details about the nightgown. I love that you were wearing her clothing when I was born. I want to know about the colour, the buttons, how it felt – did Nan think it was funny that you wore her gown when I arrived?

You awoke in the middle of the night, your belly round and skin dark brown from days laying out in the summer sun.

'You weren't meant to be born yet, Amy Lee. I was supposed to have another week. You were meant to come on Nan's birthday later that month but you came early and so fast.'

A trip to the toilet and you realised when wiping that everything was too round. You feel the pressure, and know that I am on my way. You tried to wake Dad, telling him, 'It's time.' But he wouldn't be moved; he was enjoying his sleep.

Dad starts chuckling as you tell this part of the story. He chimes in, 'No, Debra, I was awake and rubbing your lower back.'

You smile over at him, head still resting against the car door as we go around more bends.

I am six years old, and we are all giggling now.

'*Then* was I born?'

13

'No, Amy, we had to go to the hospital first, it was just around the corner, the same hospital your dad was born in.'

Dad proudly puffs out his chest as he drives; he loves that we were born in the same hospital as much as I do.

A beanbag on a hospital bed, twenty minutes, and I am there, earthside. Awabakal Land. You describe your body as a slide, and joke that I stuck my nails in as I exited, tearing, leaving you in need of stitches.

'And you loved me straight away?'

'Yes, Amy, we loved you straight away, all ten pounds of you.'

I return to laying on the back seat, smiling and holding the storying in my mind's eye. You tell me the same story, on repeat, throughout my childhood. It grows and weaves into my imagination as the ideal birth story: romanticised, relaxing in the lead-up, family around, a grandmother's nightgown, and a swift and safe exit.

Not even two decades later and I am sitting with you and Dad in the living room, my own belly round, no air conditioning, my skin red from laying in the summer heat. I lack the melanin that makes your skin glow. I rub my belly and we talk about how close we are to this baby coming earthside. I had hoped they would arrive early like I had for you, but we are now officially 'overdue'. I am exhausted.

'Mum, tell me again about the night I was born?'

'*Again?*' You laugh and begin to tell the story. You were wearing Nan's nightgown. You proceed but this time Dad isn't chuckling along and waiting to contribute like he usually would. He is watching you with a stern face.

You continue unphased, ending as always by mentioning a beanbag on a hospital bed, twenty minutes passing, and I arrive earthside.

Dad seems unhappy. He looks at my belly and back at you. He takes a deep breath.

'Don't you think it's time to tell her, Deb?'

You turn away, avoiding his gaze. I look between my parents. I am forty-one weeks' pregnant and have heard this story countless times. What don't I know?

You say nothing, and both of you sit in silence.

Dad, uncharacteristically, isn't willing to drop it. Coffee in hand, elbows on his knees, he stares at you intently.

'Why don't you tell Lou where you were when you went into labour.'

Lou is my family nickname, completely unanchored to any part of my legal name, and no-one actually knows where it began – it just simply is.

You sigh. 'I might have been pulling cones when I went into labour.'

Dad isn't satisfied. He continues to prompt you. 'And if you think about it, Deb, how long do you think you were actually in labour?'

You shoot him a glance – you aren't thrilled but concede. 'It might have been a few days … like for your grandmother, Lou.'

My belly rolls and morphs as the baby kicks around. I stare at you, my mouth agape. Your own mother had long labours, as did my aunt.

'And?' Dad stares again at you.

'And you were only six pounds, not ten.'

I sit, overheated, tired, overdue. I realise my mum didn't birth me in twenty minutes – she was so under the influence of various substances she wasn't seeing and hearing and feeling the cues her body was giving her about bringing me forth.

I have spent my whole life anticipating a swift labour, and now it dawns on me there is nothing to indicate that will be my experience.

My contractions finally begin the following week on a hot Wednesday in summer. I am wearing a floral sundress and spend that first afternoon of birth pangs eating watermelon at my parents' home on Awabakal Country.

My ten-pound baby comes earthside at 3:00 am on the Saturday, after days of labour. The same occurs again when my second baby is born.

At Christmas as we sit around the living room, new baby in my arms, I turn to my mother and say, 'Mum, tell me again about the night I was born.'

2

THE BLUE MOUNTAINS ARE HOME to many things: ancient sites, deep Dreaming, and numerous rehabilitation centres. Laying in a bed in one of these facilities, my mother, pregnant with me, wakes from a dream where she sees my father with another woman. She's convinced it's a vision, not a dream, and she sneaks out of the facility. She won't stand for it.

A trip to rehab and in that time, Dad moved *her* in. Mum got out, found out, and broke into her own home to wait. She and Aunty cut the woman's clothes up, and when the woman arrived back 'home' Mum pushed her down the stairs.

Eight months pregnant, Mum was still ready and willing to throw hands – an energy, we would later laugh, imbued to me from being within her at that time.

Did my name exist first or was it one of those cruel coincidences? Mum and Dad stayed together but when I came earthside a few weeks later, Mum wrote a new name, undiscussed, onto my birth certificate, and in place of 'father' simply wrote 'unknown'. She used her last name instead of his, a small moment of revenge.

When I ask her how she chose 'Amy' in place of the longer elegant name that she and Dad had selected – had spoken over me in her belly all those months and turned out his 'mistress' happened to share – she said it was just a name she thought I could learn to spell easily in kindergarten. Just three letters. A-M-Y.

My naming and misnaming would weave itself into my life, and shape my experiences in ways my parents could never have anticipated.

A few years later a big loss hit our home. My younger brother was born but did not live for long. He came earthside, took to the breast, but at some point his breathing stopped and they simply whisked him away to the bowels of the hospital. They never brought him back.

Mum was left with empty hands and an aching heart. She received his little ankle bracelet, a photo of him, and was told to move on. It was *over, done with,* and somehow taboo to acknowledge him or grieve. With no support for her immense grief, Mum broke. Broke down. Too many people asking, 'How much longer until that baby will be born?' Then shunning her when she tried to mumble that actually he had been born, but he no longer lived.

Dad was away, serving eight years in prison for armed robbery – Mum pregnant with my brother when he was arrested. So he was left to grieve alone in lock-up over state lines, and she was left with two girls and a hole in her heart where Michael lived still. And when it got too much for her, she was smart enough and brave enough to take herself to the hospital and tell them she was not safe.

I was in the car too, and toddled in beside her when she arrived at the hospital. Whether it was her state or Dad's incarceration, or perhaps my appearance or the fact she is a Murri woman, I do not know, but they wouldn't listen when she explained that her father, my grandfather, was on the way to collect me.

Instead they sent for social services, and they organised my removal.

In a time before mobile phones, my pop had no idea he was racing against social services as he journeyed the route to the hospital. As fate – or rather traffic flows – would have it, Pop arrived at the same time as the people who were there to take me.

The fire that raged in Pop's belly as he realised what was happening that day still burns in his eyes: it comes up whenever the mess of my name is mentioned. He recognised that the people approaching me were there for my removal, and that he would need to fight.

Pop grabbed me, barely three years old. He got me in his arms but outnumbered by hospital staff and social services – threatened with the appearance of security and police – he couldn't leave. I was his, and he was mine, and my mum had

willed that I go with him: it was arranged, she had called, that
was how he knew, that is why he came.

Still the staff were adamant and confident of their position
in the argument that ensued. Yet before security was called,
they revealed their error, the hospital's error, which all linked
back to Dad's error and infidelity: they referred to me as Amy
Teerman.

And that was never my name, not legally.

My mother kept no secrets from Pop, so he knew that my
name was not legally Amy Teerman. The hospital staff's claim
was invalid on a child who did not legally exist. Pop made
his connection clear with the simple showing of his driver's
licence. I was Amy Maccoll, my mother is Debra Maccoll, he
is Malcolm Maccoll. Holding me tightly, he left, yelling that
we were going and there was no way in hell we would wait
for them to produce the paperwork that he still feared would
disappear me.

Because I am of him, and he is of me. Our names were proof
enough; the hospital staff stepped aside. The name Mum gave me
out of anger, and a wish that I would have ease in kindergarten,
meant I stayed with my sister, with our grandparents, until she
was well again, or at least well enough to come home.

And on it went. When kindergarten enrolment came, they
didn't require a birth certificate – and why confuse a child or

highlight their difference – so they just enrolled me as Amy Teerman, a name that claimed my father and linked me to my already-enrolled sister. They did throw in a sweet middle name 'Lee', which they claimed was short for 'Cecily', my nan's name. A beautiful lie.

A lie that grew into my identity: Amy Lee Teerman, on every report, and eventually my Commonwealth Dollarmite student banking account. Because even in the poorer schools, where the kids lived in homes where ends hardly meet, the pressure to bank weekly was on.

When I moved into high school, I won awards, I gained glowing report cards, I added the occasional gold coin to that bank account, all under the name that was never actually mine. It grew and grew until the disconnect between who I was and my legal name was made clear. As I entered the workforce, the mess was not able to be cleaned up because none of us had the money to file legal documentation to change my name to match my identity.

It's only a big deal if you make it one, Amy, Mum would remark when I would rage. And so, as with so many elements of my childhood, it was their mess but I was the one who had to live with it.

I didn't yet understand the gift of protection the name had offered me that day at the hospital, or that my parents were just doing their best in moments of overwhelm.

Years later, when the day came that I married, I wasn't thinking of feminism, or family pride in names, or legal markers to bloodlines. I was thinking how nice it would be to no longer be regularly reminded of a name that is seeded in my father's infidelity, and linked with stories of trauma and pain. I was thinking of how much I love my stepdaughter and how, although we are not bonded in blood, we could be bonded in name. I was thinking of what was best for me, and *my* family, at that time. And so I told that husband I would agree to take his name, but should the day come where we divorced, I would keep it: I would publish under that name; it would become and remain mine.

So when people ask me why I chose to take on that name, when they throw shade at my identity because of this, I feel ready to throw hands like my mum did that day in the stairwell; because it would be easier than explaining the story and trauma of what is in a name.

3

THERE ARE TIMES WHEN I am asked a question and I must make a choice between lying or sharing trauma. For the longest time I didn't know it was a choice – I believed I just had to be honest and direct. The words would spill forth and I would think everything was going okay but inevitably the listener's face would drop and morph from curiosity into fear, pity, horror: all the things you don't want to see in the face of a lover or friend or colleague. While the asker clearly anticipates a sweet or fun story, my truth is often neither. My response exposes my reality and the kind of trauma that isn't visible at first glance.

What is your first memory? I was asked this once on a date. Eighteen and still overly honest, I answer.

I am a small child, no older than two, standing atop the stairs in our housing commission townhouse. I would often play on the landing of the staircase, imagining each stair to be a level within a castle for my dolls, who are of course all royalty.

My family are home, it is almost dusk, and all seems well when Dad appears at the bottom of the stairs and asks if we would like to go to the shop with him. Mum is staying home this time, so we have a choice. My older sister, Lisa, all rosy cheeks and blonde curls, bounds from her room and joins me in running down the stairs and out the front door to the orange Volkswagen Beetle in the driveway.

It's a quick trip, and now we are driving home as the stunning pink and orange hues of the late afternoon sky show through the windows, filling the car with golden light. We sing along to music playing on the radio, soft drink on our lips, and our car slows and stops at the traffic lights.

Without warning the golden light dims and we are plunged into shadow. Glancing out of the window I am confused to see we are suddenly surrounded by large vehicles. They tower over our VW Beetle, their doors sliding open, and people are jumping out, clad in dark protective gear, carrying large guns and swarming. They are everywhere: it feels like a reverse clown car situation with lots of men trying to get in.

They move with a combination of chaos and precision, guns aimed at us, and my initial confusion swiftly turns to terror as I watch our father open his door and get out of the vehicle with his hands in the air. I sense myself start screaming, and my sister and I watch on as his body is grabbed and thrown to the ground. Guns now aimed squarely at his head.

Still in the back seat, Lisa and I cry and scream. Our faces pressed against the windows of our tiny orange Beetle as the traffic lights change to green but no vehicle moves. My father turns his head slightly and his eyes lock on mine and I can see his mouth opening but can't hear what he's saying above our screaming.

They force my father into one of the vans and an armed, gear-clad officer climbs into the driver's seat of our car. We do not stop screaming as he drives us back to our home.

Once there, Lisa and I are made to sit on the footpath outside our townhouse as more cars and officers arrive and neighbours peer through windows. We sit and watch as officers pour out of their cars and vans and file into our home. The house is ripped apart from the inside out before the officers leave and we can re-enter.

On reflection, it wasn't exactly a straightforward answer for my date, but to be fair they went on to tell me a story about using crackers to blow up a myna bird's nest. So maybe neither of us were very smooth operators.

4

I N ADULTHOOD, MY HOME IS an old, small, former housing commission house on Awabakal Country. It is missing roof tiles at the front and completely without guttering at the back: signs of decades of low-to-no maintenance. But it's more than roomy enough for me and my children.

The family has taken to gathering in my carport and the yard has enough space for me to slowly be building up the garden of my dreams.

'You sure you want to plant it here, Lou?' my dad asks.

'Yeah, Dad, think about it. When it grows full size the branches will reach out to the street and the neighbours can help themselves to lemons without having to come into the yard.'

Dad nods and gets back to digging the hole, while I crouch on the grass, gently easing the citrus trees I have just brought home out of their cheap plastic pots. Dad hates physical labour when he can avoid it; he is getting old, but he's proper proud that I own my own house, so I can usually rely on him to come and help me with these kinds of things, or to lock the chooks up when I am away for work.

The citrus trees planted and watered, we wash up and I head inside to put the kettle on while Dad settles into the old armchair under the carport.

'What are these?' Dad yells out.

I glance out the window and see he is pointing at the new bluetooth speakers I have set up. Smiling to myself, I turn music on and the sound up, rather than answering him. A new band that my younger sister, Taylah, has gotten me onto begins to play, their vocals filling the carport as I fill the coffee mugs with boiling water.

Stinging for a stiff drink in a short glass

I walk out to the carport, two hot mugs of coffee in hand.

Junkies and cop cars rushing past

I almost drop the mugs, the hot liquid spilling out and over my hands. I hadn't listened to this song yet and I wasn't expecting that kind of language. *Junkies.* I place the mugs on the table and head back inside to the controls, switching to a different band.

Dad doesn't comment – he might not have even noticed the lyrics but I did. I always do. When my family are dehumanised, I feel dehumanised too. We drink our coffee and Dad begins pointing out the ways I need to improve the garden drainage but I am only half listening.

When I am little we live in a small brick townhouse set within a quiet cul-de-sac on Dharug Country. I absolutely adore this home. It's basic housing commission but to me it feels whole: finished, clean and safe.

We have neighbours who are mostly our friends and who would inevitably be described as a 'diverse community' by outsiders. Kids here ride bikes not for pleasure but because we've no resources to learn to drive, or no cars to drive if we had found the money for licensing. Bikes also allow for easy escapes from security, police and bigger kids with grievances or anger they wish to misplace.

There's a French bakery down the road near the train station, where we sometimes get warm rolls in the morning, and we are only a short drive from my grandparents – my mum's parents – so we see them all the time. We have a hearty brown dog named Dozer, and there are small purple blooms in the tiny front garden.

Some afternoons when Mum is in a good way she disappears into the kitchen to cook dinner. Lisa runs off to play with the kids on our street, and I can alternate between watching my favourite *Cinderella* videotape and sitting in the front window watching the road for the return of my father.

The streetlights coming on will mark Lisa's need to come home, and then Dad will appear, dropped off at the corner and walking down our street, esky in hand, big boots on. Lisa and I race to him – she from the street and me from the house – and he will rush forward and throw whoever reaches him first high into the air with ease, better than any rollercoaster. Though Dad will often have had long days in the sun – little more in the esky than an old cordial bottle filled with water, and unexpected parole officer visits that sometimes lead to loss of work – all I saw in those moments was his joy to be seeing us, to be home.

My dad is many things – a roofer, a labourer, a partner, a convicted bank robber – and to me he is a teacher and a translator in a world I sometimes struggle to understand. When we garden together he draws my attention to the flowers, and specifically the bees, instructing me to observe the way they hover over the blooms, collecting the pollen and going on to make honey.

As a child I will eat several of those purple flowers before he realises I have misunderstood his lesson on pollination.

Though the house is tiny, the linen cupboard is filled with books, the air is regularly filled with music and our mother is always reading, and sometimes dancing. We watch NRL as a family, always barracking for the Bunnies; we stay up late to watch documentaries on orcas, plants, lions and more, where we learn about the circle of life together. My parents don't seem to believe in censoring what we watch and so I see it all: guts and gore, death and life.

I learn many lessons in that home, sometimes intentional, sometimes through the rapid shifting of environments that waver between storm and peace.

Out the back of this townhouse there is a pergola draped in a green screen to protect from the intense summer sun, and a barbecue made of red brick. A small vegetable patch where Dad grows plants you can and can't find at a local nursery, and a clothesline where Dad pegs a pillow, which he holds as he teaches my sister and me how to punch, our thumbs correctly placed to avoid broken bones.

Never tolerate disrespect: it isn't just about that person, it's about everyone watching on, he often tells us.

Dad talks to us as my sister and I take turns hitting the pillow. Sometimes he stops to correct our stance, our technique, but mostly he praises and encourages us.

Life is a series of systems, Lou. You can move and survive anywhere if you understand respect, relationship and reciprocity.

These lessons are taught with words but also with role modelling.

When I tire of punching, Dad focuses on Lisa's technique; she is older by five years and has better endurance. I sit on the grass and Mum helps me fill up my tiny doll pool, playing with my Barbies as my sister moves with agility, her effort audible. *Ouss, ouss.*

Every year when it comes time for school holidays my parents will argue about where to spend them: Dad will say north to his family but inevitably Mum wins and we head south to hers, to Yuin Country and Great-Grandma Lucy's home. Hers is the kind of home that feels warm, lived in, and has been built by many hands over several years. Pop Maccoll and his father-in-law had been responsible for much of the construction, many moons before we kids came earthside.

The air is salty there, and whether it is Easter or Christmas there will be more cousins than beds – we will all sleep spread out in the lounge room – and it will be gloriously fun. Ignored by the adults, we will run around together all day, swimming down the river, fishing with Pop, and playing in the sandy backyard, coming inside only to find food or to escape the mosquitoes when the sun goes down.

Pop cuts up apples for us kids to feed to the possums, and Dad plays card games with my uncles; those uncles are my mother's brothers, and they played footy with my dad back in the day, so there's layers of relationship and connection here. Everyone will sing and yarn together, and Mum will disappear into the front room to dive into the rows and rows of books that line the walls – Mum's idea of heaven.

Here, we are seen. Here we belong; and it is within these moments, spaces and places that life and childhood are blissfully good.

Lisa and I spend our early years moving freely between the homes and gardens in our street; latchkey kids sharing cooked corn and rice at kitchen counters, raiding our friends' mothers' wardrobes to explore fashion and cultural garments, and building cubbies in small garden sheds and shrubberies.

When the rain rolls in and doesn't stop for days, leaf litter and rubbish build up blocking the drainage and creating a shallow pool where the street used to be. Though Mum forbids us from playing in the stormwater when her bouts of depression and Dad being locked up overlap, my sister and I are able to slip away unnoticed. We join the rest of the neighbourhood kids in swimming, splashing, and getting filthy in the closest thing we ever had to a local community pool.

We leave that townhouse and community permanently when I am seven but those lessons about respect are forever.

5

THE ENERGY OF ACADEMIC CONFERENCES isn't like your average conference. It is the bringing together of academics from universities all around the country, sometimes around the globe, all working within similar or related specialisations. This means one thing: niche gossip and lots of it. There's a reason why so many academics love reality television – we have intensely intellectual, oftentimes dry jobs, meaning much of the juicy elements of our roles come from the interpersonal relationships.

At conferences you may sit across from someone who is later on your grant or hiring panel. Though there is, of course, no formal segregation anymore, exclusions and separations based on class, race, and privilege continue.

Presentations by Indigenous academics are often attended by almost entirely Indigenous audiences, and when the proceedings break for lunch we tend to find one another out on the grass somewhere, sitting in the shade, catching up on everyone's business. Indigenous academic gossip is different though; many of us are connected through bloodline or marriage, and informal gatherings within formal proceedings allow us to check in on each other's relations, and keep atop of the cultural safety (or lack thereof) in different institutions and teams. These are the kind of yarns you wouldn't put in emails.

Learning the rhythm, language and protocol of the academy was a difficult journey. I relied on Indigenous academics to be my guides, to steer me through engagements that instead of allowing me to succeed because of what I do know, would rather see me penalised based on what I didn't.

My first academic conference is on Kaurna Country, Adelaide. Work flies me over and I am so excited, I almost bounce into the hotel on the first day. But by the end of that first day, I am deflated.

During the niceties of mingling and meeting I find myself standing within a gathering of mostly white academics and am asked:

'Is this your first time here in Adelaide?'

'No, I lived here for a while as a kid.'

'Oh, really? What was that for?'

'Dad had work here so we moved over as a family for maybe six months, a year.'

'Where did you live?'

These academics must be from here.

'Yatala.'

I answer without thinking too much about it. I haven't been here in twenty years but that name sounds about right. Yet with my answer, the energy of the small group shifts. I can tell in their faces and in my belly that I have erred, that I am erring, and I am not sure how.

An Indigenous man in the small group, who doesn't know me but clearly does realise what I have done, chimes in: 'Nah, you lived in the city, sis. I think you got the names a bit mixed up there.'

There's a release of tension – everyone laughs awkwardly – and when the crowd disperses my colleague quietly tells me Yatala is the name of the prison. The maximum-security prison.

'One of your parents in lock-up?' he asks gently.

I feel the hot blush rise from my chest and spread across my face as I nod.

'Just say you lived in the city – don't let the gubbas get you down.'

I call Mum when I am back in my room that night. She laughs at the story and reminds me we lived in Elizabeth. Then her tone changes and she asks me not to bring it up again; she wants to blank it.

'Did anyone comment on your clothes?' Mum asks, changing the subject. She volunteers in an op-shop and over the past year has been gathering professional business clothes for me whenever they come into the shop in good condition and in my size.

'Yeah! Actually a woman complimented me on my dress today, it's the pretty floral one you got me, Mum.'

She is pleased and on that note we hang up. I slip out of my gifted $3 dress and go to bed but I don't sleep. I am so cross at myself. I am not embarrassed that my dad was in lock-up; I am shamed that I said the wrong thing, that I wasn't in control with my response. I am overwhelmed with the sense that I do not belong here, that the academy is not for me, and I am not for it.

This spiral sends me emotionally back to when I was a child, and I was forever confused and often accidentally saying the wrong thing. To when I didn't know it was a prison we were visiting Dad in because everyone taught me he was simply at 'work'.

I fly home at the end of that conference but I'm still caught in that mental loop, thinking back to the time we spent on Kaurna Country as kids, remembering when our only way there and back was driving.

Dad is locked up for much of my very early childhood and during that time I really don't have a whole understanding of prisons, or how different our family is from others. I understand and have witnessed the violence of police – but the end point of that process is lost on me – the idea that adults would be forcibly caged is not a concept I have been introduced to.

In fact, it is something my family try actively to shield me from. The lie of Dad being at 'work' leaves me with a confused but naive understanding of what is happening when we visit Dad in prison. As a child I may not understand why these places scare me, though they do and I resent the fact that Dad can't leave. But that is far better than carrying the full knowledge that my dad is caged. It also means that when I inevitably talk when I shouldn't, people outside of our family won't know Dad has been away in lock-up; they too will be led to think he is away for work.

All I know is that Dad's 'workplace' is in a place called Adelaide; while he is there, he isn't allowed to come home. When we visit, it is a really, really, long drive. And when we arrive at the 'worksite' we have to pass through lots of tall fences, doors, and various checkpoints. While we wait to be processed through the metal detectors, I notice that some of the people who work here have guns.

No-one is friendly, and as eager as I am to see Dad, this place is a bit scary. We don't get to take any possessions in with us and Mum has to hand over her bag before we can go in. When we finally get to be in the same room as Dad, I think he looks handsome in his all-green uniform. Everyone in that room, talking with their loved ones, is wearing prison greens. Green like my mum's eyes.

The car splutters to a stop, overheating, as we are driving overloaded, long distance to our new home interstate. South Australia, Kaurna Country. The car seems to be matching Mum's erratic energy, which has also become lulled right before the car rolled to a stop. I've given up trying to work out what we are doing.

Before we left, Mum had thrown some of our belongings into the car and announced that we were moving to be closer to Dad. Maybe because I am so young, three years old, maybe four, and maybe because I never know when or how to keep quiet, everyone around me refers to Dad as being 'away for work'.

It's been a while since the police took him away, and we miss him terribly, and even more since my baby brother died. The distance between our home and where Dad is based is a fifteen-hour drive each way and Mum has had enough. We can't afford flights and she can't keep driving back and forth with us kids – it's time to move there.

Saying goodbye to our grandparents was hard. I don't want to be away from Pop. I belong in his home, in the mulberry tree picking fruit to eat and squish between my fingers. I belong with him, and lately he has been picking me up a few mornings a week and taking me to the pool. He has to do physio for his back. If I wait patiently on the side of the pool while he does his exercise, he then brings me into the water, teaching me how to kick and move my arms so I can keep my head above the water.

Pop, Mum's dad, is my safe person: consistent, kind, calm.
I am with him a lot, sometimes swimming, often fishing. He
takes me away to his own mother-in-law's, to Great-Grandma
Lucy's house on Yuin Country, where we fish every morning
and he tells me all about our kin creatures who live in the
river. The octopuses there are cheeky and steal our bait. I
don't want to be away from him, and I could tell by his face
as Mum told him we were leaving that he was worried. He
kept shooting glances at me and Lisa – I don't want him to
be worried.

Now, on that long drive to Adelaide, when we eventually
get the car back on the road again, Mum alternates between
muttering to herself and singing along to Patsy Cline's *Crazy*.
I am bored, carsick, and already missing my pop. Moving house
is horrible and I think maybe I hate it.

When we arrive at the new home, I can't help but think it
looks and smells funny. The carpets are all weird bright colours;
my sister takes the room with the orange carpet, mine is purple.
There are no curtains in the windows, and that first night, with
the moonlight filtering through the branches of the old tree
that scrapes against my window, I become convinced that if I
move, something that is waiting will see me and gobble me up.
I lay still in my new bed and by morning I have wet it, soaking
through the sheets and my pyjamas. Mum is disappointed but

not as much as I am disappointed in myself. I will be starting at a new preschool and I don't want the other kids to think I am a baby – only babies wet their beds.

Over the coming weeks we build a bit of a routine in that new house. Some days Mum doesn't wake up or get out of bed. With no family close by to come around and help, I soon discover that though I am not tall enough to reach the cupboards, if I open the cutlery drawer I can use it like a step to climb atop the kitchen benches. From there I can get to the Weetbix and bowls. The first few times I attempt to pour my own milk, I make a big mess and do a clumsy and loud job of cleaning up, but this doesn't wake Mum and I eventually get the hang of it. If Mum is still asleep, I will have Weetbix for lunch too, and play while I wait for Lisa to walk home from big school.

On the days when Mum does wake up, I go to preschool. Always, before we get out of the car, Mum reminds me that we are in Adelaide because Dad is here for work.

'Work, Amy, do you understand?'

'Yes, Mum.'

I am suspicious and she can tell but I don't want to do or say the wrong thing. Whenever families are spoken about at preschool, I make sure I mention Dad is at 'work'. I like being at preschool. There is a small kitchen but it isn't like the one at home where everything is too big and I have to do things alone. Here the benches are real low and there are grown-ups who help us learn to make and butter our own toast. It feels like a very empowering place to be.

Each day that we are there, all of the children are expected to have naps. Green camping beds are brought out from the storage closet and everyone lays on their own bed, quickly drifting off to sleep. I have never been made to have naps before and am not in the habit of sleeping during the day. So I remain awake and often chat to my neighbours.

The educators quickly work out that small acts of bribery are the most effective way to get me to comply with instructions and we soon come to an understanding. When the camp beds are brought out, so too is a little white paper bag with a couple of lollies inside. One of the teachers will quietly place the bag in my chunky little hand, and with a wink reminds me that if I am quiet for all of nap time, then I can secretly eat the lollies when everyone wakes up. Every day I lay quiet and still, lolly bag hidden within my fist, held under my pillow for nap time, and in the chaos of pack-away time I eat my treats with gusto.

Being in this new neighbourhood means we are able to visit Dad regularly but some of the people around our new home make me uncomfortable. Sometimes I get hurt and there isn't an adult around to help me. I miss our townhouse, the toys we had to leave behind, and my grandparents, especially fishing with Pop.

We don't last that long in Adelaide, not quite a year. Then Mum packs up the car and we drive back to our townhouse on Dharug Country. I am glad to be back with our community, to be back with Pop. Not until I am almost six years old does Dad come home for good and we all live together in the townhouse again.

As soon as Dad is home, I begin to beg my parents for a little sister. I believe in my heart of hearts that if I can have a little sister, she will be my best friend. Within the year they conceive Taylah, who comes earthside on Dharug Country.

A couple of years later I watch a movie on the violence of prison systems – I am too young for it but I had been left home alone and it was on the television. In my naivety, I still don't realise that prison is where Dad was when we say he was at work, so I simply store away the information from that movie.

Sometime after I'm out on a drive with Dad; we talk about anything and everything when we are in the car alone together. I tell him all about the grown-up show about prisons I had watched, and comment that maybe people in this country who go to jail should just be killed like they are in America because jail seems like such a rotten place.

Dad is so shocked by what I have said that the car swerves across the road momentarily, and as he restores his face and the car to the right side of the road, that's when it clicks: I realise all those times we were visiting Dad at 'work' he was in fact in prison. I feel horrible for what I said, and begin to think about the violence I saw in that movie, and how that must have been what it was like for Dad.

As a teenager, after seeing Dad regularly leaving the toilet with an empty coffee cup, I begin to chide him about how disgusting I think it is when he reads and drinks his coffee on the toilet. Dad and I regularly engage in playful but intense arguments, and I am getting better at annihilating him in them.

'How is drinking coffee in there any different to when the toilet is next to your bed in a cell?' he retorts, confident in his argument.

'Dad, I would say the difference is: this isn't prison. No-one's trying to punish you. Go drink your coffee in the sun.'

Touché.

6

T HE HOUSE LIGHTS FLASH, SIGNALLING it's time to take our seats. Setting down my half-finished glass of white wine, which I hated but drank to fit in, I move with the other parents, carers and grandparents out of the foyer and into the theatre. We weave between one another, exchanging excited smiles, checking tickets and putting phones on silent.

All year we've been diligently bringing our young ones to their weekly ballet classes, waiting together in the family room (we weren't allowed to watch practice), and paying the rather substantial fees and costume charges. The price is a bit of a stretch for me and I can't take time off for the classes, so I take my laptop and work while I wait. Occasionally I listen in to the other parents as they discuss subjects, brands and predicaments I don't generally understand. This is their world – I am just visiting – but I do my best not to let them know that. Tonight is the end of year recital, and our children will be performing *The Nutcracker*.

I sink into a plush red theatre seat, the air is refreshingly cooled and I like the way the sound is muffled by thick curtains and carpeting. This place feels expensive.

The lights go down, leaving us sitting in darkness. Music begins to play and my breath catches unexpectedly in my chest as the curtains open, and the first of the older ballerinas move across the stage. I've never seen ballet in person before. The music starts to swell, and so does my heart. By the time it's my child's turn to be pointing their toes and twirling on stage, my eyes are streaming.

I feel embarrassed to be crying but the force of my emotions has caught me completely off guard. I am grateful for the dark and the anonymity it provides. I'm proud of my child, moved by how beautiful the entire production is, but I'm also feeling deep grief. As a child myself, I longed for – I still long for – these moments for me, and they've always been out of reach. There are adult ballet classes, I have seen them on the schedule but my time and my budget won't stretch that far. I can afford one set of classes and costumes, and they're not for me.

Though I am completely filled up with love, pride and joy at seeing my baby on stage, tightly woven within those same feelings are a mix of ugly, raw ones – jealousy, anger, sadness – there is no separating them. The complexities of parenting and dreaming in the present, while processing my own trauma and past, are hard sometimes.

I take deep breaths, running my fingers along the velvety material of the theatre seats, wiggling my toes and focusing my eyes on the dancing as I try to ground my body in the moment. To sit in this time and not in my own childhood, to embrace my privilege as mother, even while acknowledging my disadvantage as a daughter. When the curtains close, we all dramatically jump to our feet, a standing ovation for our children.

Her hand tugs on mine willing me to move, but my feet are planted, eyes transfixed on the shop window. Mannequins pose in impossible positions, displaying an array of tutus and dance costumes. They look amazing – I want to be just like them, a ballerina: pretty, poised and graceful.

Mum pulls on my hand again, and this time I lift my feet, following her as we walk hand in hand up the street to her work at the computer store. It is a simple store on a bustling main street. While she works I sit behind the glass counter, drawing on scraps of paper until lunch when we walk down to the local corner shops.

At a café Mum orders toast, extra burnt, and requests in detail that they must apply the butter as soon as they remove the toast from the toaster. I order a strawberry milk and a sandwich with white bread, butter, and shredded chicken. Nothing more and nothing less.

We are in a good season, one with rhythm and resources, and this is my favourite part of the day. Mum and I sit together, and as we eat she talks to me about anything and everything that is on her mind. Today she is explaining to me that every person who exists is, in and of themselves, a world of possibilities.

'Amy, do you ever just look at someone and wonder about their life? They could be anyone, anything; if you sit and watch people you can see the unlimited possibilities of this world.'

I am not quite school age yet. So no, the concept of people existing as multifaceted creations, each with boundless and countless potential beyond my own experience has not yet occurred to me.

'I wonder what decisions they made that brought them to this place and space in time.'

Mum is looking over her tea, watching a young professional pair who are ordering at the sandwich counter. As she looks at them, I think she *looks* kind of how I *feel* when I stare at the shopfront of the dance store: filled with longing.

'Mum, can I do dancing? I want to be a ballerina.'

'Sure, Amy, not a problem.'

In that moment, Mum consents with her words and I am elated. But her words aren't often followed with any kind of consistent action.

Over the following years, on occasion Mum will take me to dance classes. I will be enthusiastic and engaged, listening to the teacher as I stand in bare feet and casual clothes amongst the children in their leotards and top buns. Mum will assure the teacher that the *following* week we will return in dance uniform, and with the term payment. The teacher and I will both believe her. But we never return. Trial classes is all I ever get. There is always money for cigarettes and heroin but never for leotards, stockings, dance shoes or term fees.

As I grow, I am jealous of the other girls at school who go to dance in the afternoons. And when we visit our dad's mum, Grandmother Teerman, I look with envy at the framed photographs she has on display of my cousins at their recitals. Their hair tied back, tutus and lipstick on. I don't want to take what those other girls have; I just want to join them where they stand on pointed toes. Their world of possibilities is somehow so different from my own. Their dads aren't in jail, and their mums don't work in strange offices and pubs.

The closest I get to ballet is a bag of hand-me-down dance costumes passed along one day from a cousin. Opening the bag, a rainbow of colour – tulles, satins and sequins – spill in front of me. I run my hands through the beautiful mess. I wear those costumes for days on end, pointing my toes and twirling myself from room to room. I know I am not elegant or poised; I wonder how the Disney princesses in my favourite movies, though never taught how to dance, somehow know exactly how to move and hold themselves when they come face to face with their prince. Glass slippers never misstep.

As I stand in front of the bathroom mirror, I see that I can't make my body look the way it does in the ballets I have seen on television. But the material feels heavenly on my skin. And if I close my eyes as I leap between furniture, even though I am just a little girl in public housing with a daddy in lock-up, I can easily imagine I am on a stage — tutu on, dancing in a life of different possibilities.

THROUGHOUT MY CHILDHOOD I OFTEN perceive life as a series of battles. Physical, psychological, systemic: we are under attack. The peace of our family and home is regularly disrupted by police, raids, addiction, incarceration, debt collectors, poverty and some days it feels obliterated by the constant blows rained upon us. As a child I live within those battles, seeing them, experiencing them, but having no power to act against them, to contribute to my own safety or that of my family and community.

But in school, things are different. In class I feel empowered, I learn quickly. If there are fights here, I know I can win, and win them I do. I am rewarded with praise, words of encouragement, stamps, stickers, a place in the Gifted classroom. When it comes to formal learning, when I am assessed I am not found to be wanting. I realise early on that though I often feel overwhelmed, if I persist with school I might discover and create the tools and resources I need to fight for my family, for myself, for our community. Find a way to keep and protect our homes and bodies, to actively take back space so we might thrive. Education is power.

When we return from Adelaide back to Dharug Country and my grandparents, I am so excited for big school that I plead with my mother in the lead up to Christmas to take me to the doctor for my shots. I want to go to school in the new year and Nan says I have to get vaccinated before I can go. As scared as I am of needles, I beg Mum to organise to take me to get them.

She does, and we go together. I accept the needle with the kind of stoic attitude that makes the GP comment that I am surely the bravest of children and this makes me happy. Mum treats me with a lolly from the little store next to the medical centre as we walk back to Nan and Pop Maccoll's home.

When the day finally arrives that I can go to big school, I change my mind. We are gathered at Nan and Pop's house, lunches packed, bags at the front door, when suddenly my intense excitement turns to horrid anxiety. As my older sister walks out the front door, I panic. I don't want to go! I want to stay home with Pop. I begin to scream and carry on, literally dropping to the floor and holding on to the kitchen chair leg, as my mother tries to drag me to the front door.

Eventually, hair in two plaits, blue-checked school dress on and two hours late, I am willing to walk into the kindergarten room. Lisa is already in her class, across the quad. That first day Mum walks me in, I am introduced to my teacher, Ms Walker, and she shows me where I will sit. Then I go choose some toys to play with from the shelves. As I do, I notice a small blond boy crying. I come to think of him as crying Thomas because unlike me he continues to cry most days at school, whereas I fall in love with being there.

The second day, it is Pop who walks me into kindy, and we discover that he knows my kindergarten teacher's father. The next day, I walk myself into class but I carry a letter my grandfather has written, handing it to my teacher who then passes it on to her own father. After that she goes from being friendly to very warm and caring towards me. I feel like I am her favourite – a great teacher can make every child feel like their favourite. I make friends quickly, and my first crush at big school is a quiet girl with long, light brown hair.

Though I love being at school, one week I have a massive meltdown in class – I cry even more than Thomas. I do not care if any of the other kids see. I am infuriated by a great, big, dirty red line that has been placed straight through the word 'terrarium' in my daily journal entry. The ink is as dark as the all-encompassing rage that swells up within me, and while I don't recall when I started screaming I do recall the look on Ms Walker's face as she rushed back into the room. She had been elsewhere, leaving the class in the care of a student teacher, who was adamant that I had misspelt the word 'terrarium' in my journal.

On the weekend we went to Nan and Pop's house and they gave me a terrarium which my Pop made for me.

I had drawn a glass terrarium, complete with the plants I imagined I would grow within it. My chunky little five-year-old self approached the desk to show this stand-in fake student teacher my work, as was the routine in our class, only to witness her whip out that red pen and obliterate my creation as she sat in the chair of my favourite teacher.

The outrage was immediate. She had RUINED my journal entry with her own inability to spell. I argued with her. Her authority was nothing. She was not my REAL teacher, and as soon as I saw the red pen in her hand, I had told her: 'STOP! NO!' But she didn't listen and with the damage now done, I had stood there and screamed until Ms Walker came rushing back in.

My wonderful, warm, understanding kindy teacher approaches the desk where I stand with clenched fists and red face, and looks at my page as I explain through tears what has happened. The student teacher shakes her head dismissively, as Ms Walker's eyes scan my page. I know in this moment that I am right. She shoots daggers at the student teacher who looks confused in return. Vindication.

That is when Ms Walker takes the opportunity to teach me one of the most valuable lessons I will ever learn. She doesn't address the student teacher, turns her back on her slightly and says, 'Amy, did you know there is a way to check spelling?'

I did not know. I just assumed all adults magically knew how to spell.

'There is a book called a dictionary. It has all the words you might want to use and you can find them to check your spelling.'

Amazing. Brilliant. I needed one. She again shoots daggers at the student teacher as she pulls a book from the shelf, and after opening it explains that the system is known as 'alphabetical order' and together we went through the Ts until we came to the word 'terrarium'.

T-E-R-R-A-R-I-U-M.

There it was. I was right.

The student teacher, who had been sitting there quietly while we went on this journey through the workings of a dictionary, mumbled something. Maybe an apology, which in my heart I definitely did not accept. I wiped my snotty face on my sleeve.

We couldn't erase the red, but in that moment, I understand that tools do exist that can prove when we are right, even when the person we are arguing with is older, stronger, and holding the red pen.

8

THE ROAD SNAKES AHEAD OF me between green and gold earth – it rises up tall and proud like my people. Tufts of white cotton cling to the grass and scrub that lines the road, mirroring the balls of white cloud that linger above in sky country. But unlike the clouds, the cotton does not belong here. It's a long drive, and the temperature begins to climb as the horizon slowly but surely flattens out. Landscape changing, spinifex abundant, as the sealed road ends. I continue along the red dirt towards the camp.

Just as I'm about to lose reception for the week a text comes in from Mum.

Drive safe, don't drive tired. Love you xx

I'll be off grid, out of reception and on Country for the whole week, and a combination of schedules and illness has meant my parents and siblings won't be coming with me. So I drive solo to the big mob gathering. We'll engage in ceremony,

connection and listening. We come together with intention –
not just to learn anew but so that our cells might be called upon
to remember.

On a regular school morning, Mum gets Lisa and me out of
bed and, still wearing our pyjamas, we drive to our Nan and
Pop Maccoll's house a few suburbs over on Dharug Country.
Jimmy Barnes will be blasting through the cassette player, the
sun not quite up. And if we are lucky, my sister and I will get
to go back to bed, this time at our grandparents' house while
our mother continues on to work.

By the time we wake again, Nan will have pressed our school
clothes and Pop will have ensured there is fresh bread, fruit and
milk in the kitchen. After breakfast I will sit on my grandparents'
bed and watch Nan as she readies herself for work. She has short
curly hair and always wears a silky slip under her uniform. I adore
Nan's details, and the way she is a woman of layers; underwear,
pantyhose, silky slip, dress, watch, lipstick, perfume all applied
and in order before she leaves for the day. I see her as being akin
to a princess or queen from the stories I obsess over.

Nan and my own mum may be mother and daughter but
they sit in stark contrast to one another. Where Mum is tall,
angular, flat-chested and brown-skinned, Nan is shorter,
curvaceous, with milky pale skin. They align as both being
women of swift correction. If you slouch in front of either of

them, expect your shoulders to be pulled backwards; if you misuse language, it won't be let go.

'I like your stockings, Nan.'

'*These aren't stockings, Amy, they're pantyhose.*'

'I am so sweaty, Nan.'

'*Are you a horse, Amy? Horses sweat, ladies perspire.*'

Unlike my mother, my nan's form gives soft, lightly scented cuddles. Her scent is a combination of perfume and lotion, and when she holds me in her lap, I feel as if I could disappear into her ample bosom, a physical trait I sadly do not grow up to inherit.

I spend most of my time with Pop – he is my best friend in the whole world – but I am lowkey obsessed with my grandmother and her belongings. There often seems to be a light tension between Nan and me – one I do not fully understand. I am *a lot*, and perhaps she needs me to *be less*, or perhaps we just speak different languages.

Also it is clearly very tiring for Nan, being the mother of my mum, having to work and always having grandchildren in her house. When she isn't home I sit in her room and play with her shoes. They're kept in a long, shallow wire basket under her dresser; all have a low heel, are elegant and some of them are strappy. I spend hours trying them on and playing with the trinkets she keeps in glass dishes on her dresser.

Any canteen money we get comes from these grandparents. They keep tins of spaghetti in the cupboard for my 'same-fooding'. We attend the school around the corner from their house, rather than the one closest to our own, so that we can walk to and from school. This way, regardless of whether Dad is locked up, or both my parents are working, there will always someone 'home' to greet and watch us kids. When parents are invited to the school for events, it is often just my grandparents who attend for us.

It is in their backyard that we play after school, helping Pop garden, listening to him talk with the magpies. Our kin creatures always surround us when we are with Pop – he reminds me that they are our friends. In the summer heat we play with the hose, spraying it in the air until rainbows appear and we are soaked through. When we accompany Nan to the shopping centre, she will give us a gold coin to pick a toy from the junk store; and after ordering a cappuccino she will sometimes let me skim the foam off the top. I grow up to love coffee not for the caffeine but for the way the aroma brings me back to those moments.

When evening comes we usually stay and have dinner with my grandparents too. Pop cooks while Nan organises our baths; afterwards she sits me in front of the small bar heater in the living room and brushes my long auburn hair before plaiting it in two braids. She is a woman of rhythm and ritual, after brushing my hair she will sit on the couch under the reading lamp moisturising her elbows, ankles and hands. Amongst the chaos and unpredictability of life with my parents, prone to arriving late and sometimes not at all, I find her rhythms to be incredibly soothing and settling.

By the time I am eight years old, Nan's own mother,

Great-Grandma Lucy, will have passed. Our family routine of travelling down the coast to her home on Yuin Country for holidays will end, and Nan and Pop will have divorced, with Nan moving away from Sydney for good.

Pop remains my best friend and guide in adulthood but it is Nan I think of as I moisturise my elbows, ankles and hands of an evening. Myself now a woman of rhythm, if not one of soft cuddles and ample bosom.

9

H ER SLIPPER FALLS OFF, LANDING on the stairs, collected by
the prince who doesn't need to use his words to show
her his deep and immediate love – he demonstrates it
instead with action. Holding on to that slipper, using all of
the resources at his disposal, he seeks her out. Though every
day is a challenge for Cinderella, this love, and the rescue
that accompanies it, comes with ease. She is passive as the
fairy godmother transforms her exterior, and again when she
is being chosen by the prince who lifts her out of a life of
poverty and servitude. All she had to do was work hard and
be kind.

As a small child living in poverty, in consistently difficult
situations, I loved the dresses and magic of fairytales. I especially

loved the *ease* of a princesses' transformation from poverty to abundance – Cinderella was my absolute favourite.

I carry my beaten-up Cinderella video with me everywhere I go and watch it on repeat at home and at my grandparents' place. Everyone is sick of it but me. When I am not watching it, I'm fantasising about living in a large castle with teams of people to help me care for the town, vaults of wealth, and closets filled with fancy dresses. I don't want to be poor anymore.

One Saturday, my video ending, I roll off of the couch at my grandparents' house and walk into the kitchen to see what Nan is doing. Mum and Dad were meant to collect me hours ago but predictably they haven't turned up. Things are particularly tense at the moment; I don't know it at the time, but Dad has been arrested once more and the lawyers are costing money and time that no-one has.

I stand barefoot on the lino floor watching my nan, who is making a cake and seems distracted. Nan spots me and passes me a mixing bowl. I do my best to stir the mix but it is swiftly taken from me. She's exasperated – I'm not doing it right. Nan stirs and stirs, staring out the window.

Sensing her distraction, I pluck up the courage to ask, 'Nan, what do I need to do to not be poor when I grow up?'

She doesn't turn around or pause, and I suspect in that moment she saw only the debt and the burden of my parents that fell so squarely on my grandparents' shoulders. She continues stirring the cake batter then mutters, 'Become a lawyer.'

'And how do I become a lawyer?' I ask.

'You go to university.'

The stirring done, she pours the batter into the pan, slides the pan into the oven and gives me a look. I take the hint and go outside.

I sit on the green metal stairs by the back door and reflect on what she said. I am maybe six years old but now I know I must, at all costs, go to university. I do not know anyone who has been to university, but I also do not know anyone who I would consider rich; so there seems to be a correlation there. Neither of my parents or my grandparents had the opportunity to finish high school. But from that moment onwards I am determined to complete school and go on to higher education. I will lift us out of poverty.

My fantasies shift and grow as I sit on those stairs listening to the magpies warble. I will marry royalty and I will go to university. It doesn't occur to me that both goals are statistically improbable – almost impossible – for a child like me.

10

WHEN I REFLECT UPON THE transition of moving from Dharug Country (Sydney) to Awabakal Country (Lake Macquarie) as a child, I find the memories get mixed up and overlap. My school uniforms and playgrounds changed, but it happened so gently at first that I barely realised what was happening. The move from Dharug Country to Kaurna Country (Adelaide) had been woven tightly with stress, prompted by Dad's arrest and incarceration, complicated by my brother's death, intense financial pressure, interstate trips and all the grown-ups in my life looking miserable. This move to Awabakal Country was different.

He always swore he would be done with that rubbish before he had kids, one of my aunties told me once. We were at some family event, and she was looking over at my dad who was on the nod while she said it. In that moment, as young as I was, I wondered if she spoke with the belief that I would be comforted by her comment. Or if she simply saw me, even as a child, as a safe person with whom she could vent. Either way, her comments didn't lighten my burden; they added to it.

Dad had been in and out of lock-up since before I was born, before any of us kids were born – for robbing banks, stealing – and with addiction holding him in its grip, assuring him *this won't be forever*. When he was out of jail, our home was a mixed space: relationally it was full of love but logistically the pantry and fridge were often empty.

Mum and Dad were each stuck in a vicious cycle, trapped in the push-pull of poverty and difficulties that arise from complex circumstances – some of their own making, others completely out of their control. In Sydney, on Dharug Country, we had the support of being close by to Mum's family, but we were living in a region where access to heroin was as easy as going down the street for bread and milk. Something was needed to break the cycle they were caught in – that we were all caught in.

When I am seven, an opportunity comes up – thanks to the support of Dad's parents – for him to buy into the property market. To move us out of our townhouse, out of public housing, and closer to his family. So we move two hours north, to the lands and waterways where Dad and I had both been born into: Lake Macquarie, Awabakal Country. This wasn't a perfect solution but perfect solutions don't truly exist, and addiction isn't simple; it claws, gnaws and persists. But even with addiction holding on tightly, this was a chance to build new life, and while our circumstances continued to be complex, Dad never went to jail again.

It is still dark when my older sister, Lisa, shakes me awake.

'Amy, get up. Mum's having the baby.'

'Go away, the baby isn't coming for ages!'

I try to roll over and ignore her, believing it to be nothing more than a sibling prank. Before I can successfully drift back into sleep, strange sounds from the next room begin to hit my ears and tickle at my brain. Opening my eyes, I realise there are lights on – something must be wrong because it is the middle of the night. I disentangle myself from my blankets and roll out of bed, trying not to wake my toddler sister who is snuggled in behind me.

I pad out, barefoot and confused, stopping to stand between my parents' bed and the freezer. Dad had started renovating this house as soon as he bought it, and moved us out of housing commission and up here to Lake Macquarie. But in the year we've lived here, all he has really managed to do is remove some walls; turning what was originally a neat home into a mess of confusing layout and plaster. My parents' bed stands in what was originally the living room, right beside the front door and facing the chest freezer and refrigerator, which sit in what should be an entry way.

As my eyes adjust to the light I realise that the sounds I could hear was Mum moaning. She is kneeling at the end of her bed, her back to where I now stand. Dad is by the chest freezer, landline phone in hand. He is talking to someone, but when seeing me he hands me the phone quickly and tells me that I need to take over talking to the ambulance operator so that Lisa can help him and Mum.

Nothing is ready – the baby is not meant to come for at least another six weeks – and I am still waking up as I take the receiver and begin to listen to the operator.

'Hello?'

'Hello honey, what's your name?'

'My name is Amy.'

'How old are you, Amy?'

'I am eight.'

Mum begins to moan louder and looking over her shoulder at me, says urgently, 'Tell them to hurry, Amy, the baby is coming.'

The operator explains that an ambulance is on the way. She asks me to tell her what I can see. I rub my eyes and lean against the chest freezer. I begin to explain that Mum is kneeling with no pants on, her undies down but at the halfway point between hip and knee. The floor looks wet beneath her.

'Mum, is it a boy or girl?' I ask casually.

The baby hasn't emerged but I am curious and pretty confused about what happens in birth and wonder if she can tell already.

'I don't know yet,' Mum says between moans.

'Mum, the operator wants to know what's happening? Can you look at where the baby comes out and tell me what you see?'

Dad shoots daggers at me as Mum responds.

'Amy, if I look down I will pass out!' She can't handle the sight of blood.

I can see there is a fair bit of blood running down her legs pooling beneath her.

Dad is starting to panic – I can see it in his face – while my sister looks simultaneously excited and worried. He is standing and she kneeling; one on either side of Mum, who is moaning longer and louder.

'Amy, tell them the baby is coming NOW!'

Dad runs his hands through his hair. 'It's too early for it. Ask them how long they will be!'

I can sense the fear in his voice and I begin to cry.

The operator hears me and says, 'They're on their way, Amy, they're coming as quickly as they can.'

My breathing begins to catch in my chest and I resort to begging the ambulance operator to make the doctors hurry up and help my mum. She begins to respond but I have no idea what she says because right then I am watching as an entire wet, bloodied and clearly slippery baby falls out of my mother.

There is a sudden scramble of hands as my sister and Dad reach from either side to catch him. The baby boy landing in Mum's undies and Dad's hands – just missing hitting the floor – and Mum lets out a mighty gasp.

'Towel! Grab the towels!'

Dad is shouting at my older sister. I have dropped the phone to dash forward and see the baby that is quickly being bundled up in towels and arms. Dad quietly tells Mum that she's had a boy but he isn't calm or elated. He is just quieter in his panicking now and not happy that I have left the phone.

'Amy, tell them they need to get here NOW!'

I run back to the phone and hear the operator calling down the line for me.

'Amy, can you tell me what's happening there?'

'The baby is here.'

Moments later the ambulance crew come through the door. I hang up the receiver and climb atop the chest freezer to be out of the way. I sit and watch crossed-legged as the paramedics move calmly but swiftly around my mother and new baby brother. There is a sense of fear and urgency. And soon Mum, Dad and the baby are gone – a large, bloodied mess is all that remains to show a baby had just come earthside in our home.

That baby will go on to grow into a beautiful little boy who smells like puppy dogs when he sweats and likes to sleep in my bed, nestled behind me at night. Eventually he will develop into a man who towers at almost two metres tall in adulthood. But for those first few weeks his life is touch and go; born too early, small, and in need of the neonatal intensive care team's support.

We kids visit the hospital with Dad but are unable to touch the new baby. Instead, we look at him through the clear plastic of the humidicrib. His dramatic and unexpected home birth makes the local paper. The other kids at school let me know that the news says my brother had died a record-breaking number of times in that first ambulance ride to the hospital.

Grandma, Dad's mum, comes over to help that week and I watch as she tries various chemicals and soaps to remove the stains of the afterbirth. But we soon discover that not only has it soaked through and destroyed the carpet, it has also stained beneath. Powerful stuff!

I think it looks like an entire pumpkin has been left there – deteriorated and dissolved into the wood. Unable to remove the flooring itself, instead we put the Christmas tree there that year. The plastic frame acting as a type of cover for the storying of my brother's birth caught within the floorboards.

11

I STAND LOOKING UP AT THE towering wall of bandaids in the chemist. There are too many to choose from and I am finding it confusing. My confusion must be evident as one of the women who works there approaches.

'Can I help you find something?'

'Um, yeah, I need wound dressings.' I continue looking along the shelves as I speak. 'My dad has had a heap of skin cancers removed and the stitches are pretty extensive, but also my dad is a unit, he's real big like 6 foot 5 and—'

'Amy, I know who your dad is.' The woman smiles as she interrupts.

I stop looking at the bandaids and focus on the shop assistant. Seeing her properly this time – she does look kind of familiar. I consider where I am: this is Dad's local chemist.

He comes here regularly for his scripts, his GP is right next door. He's been coming here for decades now – so of course they know Dad – and by extension that means they've known and know me. I relax, glad for the help. Dad mostly has a good relationship with the staff here, so I trust this woman will help me.

Together we gather the larger dressings and some saline. She gives me instructions on how to apply the dressing before reminding me only Dad can collect his latest script, so I will need to bring him in for that. I thank her, dash across the car park and drive to Dad's.

He isn't working at the moment – can't work – and now with the surgeries on his leg he can't really do much of anything until he's healed up. After cleaning and dressing his leg, I make us coffee while he calls his own dad to remind him I will be on the television tonight.

As well as being an academic at a university, I am a semi-regular on a news panel show; tonight they've flagged with me that the topic is incarceration. So I want to talk with Dad a bit about it before I go home to prepare. We eat biscuits together and talk about the violence of lock-up, the work of doing my thesis, how the kids are going in school, and the idea of a family trip to the zoo in the upcoming school holidays. We haven't been to the zoo as a family since I was a kid.

The crinkle of the thin plastic tray of chocolate biscuits makes me smile and hold my breath as I slide it out from its purple wrapper. As quietly as I can, I take a chocolate biscuit finger out, listening for Mum in the bathroom but there is only silence. I grin and hold the biscuit before sliding the tray back into its sleeve, and tiptoe over to the twin beds in the musty motel room we are staying in on a short trip away to visit the zoo.

My baby siblings are too young to be aware of what I am doing as I sit behind them on the floor. Max is a newborn, and Taylah isn't quite two; they are watching the motel TV. I lean up against the foot of one of the beds and feel very proud of myself for this little act of defiance.

We never go on trips anymore. As much as Dad is always talking about wanting to 'get in the car and go for a family drive' – there are six of us now – the car only seats five, so it never happens. Mum and I also get wicked carsick and even driving here we ended up taking turns throwing up – we stopped for Mum first and it was gross – and then I threw up and it was even worse.

This week Lisa is off with our cousins, riding horses or motorbikes or something fun like that but completely uninteresting to me. This means there are just five of us, so we have taken the car, booked a cheap motel and are going to the zoo tomorrow.

I am hoping to see a white tiger; they are my favourite and I borrowed a book from the school library to learn as much about them as possible. I want to see one prowl around an enclosure and have it look me in the eye. I think they are majestic and strong, and without a doubt the greatest animal in the world. I stretch my legs out in front of me, thinking about white tigers, as the chocolate finger melts a little in my hand. I am eight years old.

The bathroom door swings open and I drop my shirt sleeve over my hand to cover the biscuit that I've started eating. I stop chewing. It is a game: concealing from Mum that I snuck one of the biscuits she told me to leave 'til after dinner. She doesn't look at me, instead walking between us children sitting on the floor, and going around the bed that I lean against. I hear her sit down a bit behind me, also leaning against the bed. She says nothing.

At first, I think she is waiting to hear me crunch the biscuit so she can spring upon me. I am very still and the chocolate is melting in my mouth in a such a way that soon I'll be able to swallow without detection. I am a genius.

But then I realise that I am not the only one who is suspiciously still. I feel it first in my belly – a gnawing and growing sense of panic that spreads under my skin to my fingers and toes and the top of my crown. I can *feel* her lack of movement. Where is the breath that should be on the back of my neck, the chuckle I was waiting to hear as she caught me with the biscuit? Her signs of life are missing.

I want desperately to turn my head to look at her. I want to scream for help. I want my dad to be back from running an errand. But I am paralysed. I cannot turn my head or bring myself to look at her. My mind begins to scream at me that something is very wrong; but I am frozen, my child fingers crushing the remainder of the biscuit between my fingers as I dig my nails into my palm.

Time passes. Silence.

Finally I glance over my shoulder with the slightest twist of my neck, then cast my eyes forward again. I hope Max and Taylah won't cry or turn around. One is asleep, the other enamoured with the screen. And if it weren't for Tay's coos and chattering, and the animations that dance across the grainy television screen in front of me, I would have thought that time itself had stopped.

But only Mum's breathing has.

I have no idea how much time passes – this will be a problem later. I know better than to go for help but I also do not know what to do in the meantime. So I do nothing but hold myself as perfectly still as my little body will allow.

Finally, Dad walks in and out of my mouth tumble the words, 'Mum is asleep.'

He looks at me – my tone has alerted him.

He sees, he knows, he swings into action. 'How long has she been asleep for, Amy?'

I stand up. 'I don't know.'

He steps over to her and lifts her light body in his arms in one swooping motion. As he drops her onto the single bed against the wall, I see him pick something up from within the bundle that her body has become; it is bright orange and he moves it into his pocket. In the black and white haze of the terror I feel – the orange burns into my brain. It is the cap off a syringe.

Mum's body is now on the bed and Dad tells me to run to reception and ask them to call an ambulance. He says it calmly, firmly, but I won't move. I am standing, crying – I cannot move. He isn't looking at me, he is looking at her but he knows I haven't moved. He begins to yell at me as he compresses on her chest: one, two, three.

'Amy! Go!'

But I still don't move. She is dying; I know it, and I am terrified. He stops to bend and breathe into her. Again, one, two, three. He presses on her chest with such force that her arms flail up and down. Her arms are flapping wildly and she looks like a rag doll – lifeless under his compressions. I am transfixed.

He yells at me once more. One, two, three: 'AMY, AMBULANCE, GO, NOW!'

With every compression she looks simultaneously like she may well break under his force but also like a bird trying to take flight. So much movement but her body is also limp as he breathes into her mouth and continues compressions. Her face is empty and grey.

Dad is panicking. He turns his head and looks at me, spit flying as he screams, 'AMY, GO, NOW! TELL THEM WE NEED AN AMBULANCE!'

I am eight. I don't dare defy him any longer. I move, open the motel room door and dash across the car park. I burst through the glass door of reception and shout at the receptionist whose face I cannot see through my tears. 'Please, we need an ambulance. My mum is dying, hurry!'

They nod and grab the telephone and as soon as I am sure they understand, I am sprinting across the car park again.

I burst back into the motel room but everything has changed. Gone is the chaos of Dad compressing Mum's chest; instead, everything is still. Mum's eyes are open. She breathes. She is alive. What comes next feels worse than all that came before.

'Amy, go and tell them we don't need the ambulance,' Dad instructs me.

'No!' I may only be eight but in that moment I am defiant once more.

'Amy, go back and tell them it was a mistake – we don't need the ambulance anymore.'

I look at my mother: she is still grey. She was dying, I won't do it.

'AMY, GO!'

I go.

Across the car park once more, slowly this time, into the glass and red-brick room. The receptionist is shocked. I am just a child but they listen, and again pick up the phone. I am disappointed that they listen to me and now the ambulance won't come. Every single cell within my being is screaming at me that we need an ambulance but I do as I am told.

Again, I walk back into the motel room. I wipe my streaming nose on my sleeve and my melty chocolate hand down my shirt.

Mum is no longer in the main room. She is in the shower.

Dad tells me I have to go into the bathroom with her. I comply. The door is closed behind me.

Very quickly the tiny motel bathroom fills with hot steam; it is suffocating. Mum sits under the hot jets and I rest on the sink. She wants to know what I saw, what I know. *How will I tell this story when we are again around family?* is what she means.

I am desperate to follow the rules, and in this family, the rules change a lot. So I keep details to myself; I do not mention the orange cap, or the fact I know she died. I keep the fact that I feel overwhelmed by the shock and terror of watching and feeling her life disappear right beside me, sensing her shift from walking in front of me, to dying on the floor right behind me. Instead, I tell her anything I think she wants to hear; I just want out of this bathroom.

I wish my older sister Lisa was here; now I will have to carry this secret alone. I can't breathe. Is it because steam has filled the room and is so thick I can no longer see my mum that I drop to the floor to escape it and cannot breathe? Or is it my first anxiety attack?

I become so good at disassociating as I grow up that to this day, I do not know how much of my response was emotional and how much was physical. In that moment, I just desperately do not want to do the 'wrong' thing, so I feel out the conversation.

I watch her eyes, and her movements closely, as diminished as they are. I see she is still not completely earthside – she is in the in-between. I answer how I think she wants me to; I gently and subtly open the bathroom door to access some oxygen.

Later that day Mum and Dad teach me how to check if someone is breathing – the sounds, the sights – and impress upon me that I am responsible for being aware of the movement of a person's chest. I feel responsible for everything that has happened that day. With a combination of intense love and deep fear, for the next few years I will develop the habit of waking in the middle of most nights, panicked that their breathing will have stopped. I will creep into my parent's bedroom and listen as long as it takes for me to distinguish there are two sets of lungs moving in the darkness before I return to my bed.

The next day, we go to the zoo. I am no longer excited, and I can feel that things are 'off' and my parents' discussions exclude me. I think they are nervous, and I am worried. We come to the Sky Safari, a system of rope and pulleys that see a carriage travel a loop high above the zoo grounds, which I'm keen to go on. They are adamant that I ride alone. I am scared, it is new to me and it is so high – I hoped we could ride it together. But they insist that I get on alone; they say we can't afford more than a single rider. It costs money, everything does, and now I feel shame for pushing that we all get on.

I ride the Sky Safari alone, and they stay with the two prams. I am aware that conversations will be happening that I would benefit from hearing – confusion will become a marker of my childhood. I ride high above the zoo, in a loop of the grounds, but I spend the whole time trying to keep my eyes on Mum and Dad.

As we leave the zoo they let me pick a white tiger toy from the souvenir store. It is just a hard plastic toy, but that's not how I see it. The layer of faux fur is soft and I think it is perfect – it has pretty blue eyes that I stare into for the whole drive home.

I keep the secret of the orange cap and what happened in that musty motel room. A few weeks later I take the tiger toy into the bath with me. The hot water seeps in between the plastic and the faux fur, lifting it, disintegrating the glue in seconds until I am left holding nothing but the hard plastic, lifeless mould.

12

'EVERYONE, PLEASE STAND WHILE WE acknowledge Country and have a minute silence for our loved ones.'

We stand, gathered in a small school library, our chairs placed around the school tables, which have been pushed into the centre of the room. I am a member of the Aboriginal Education Consultative Group – a mostly volunteer body who are also collectively the peak advisory body to the state and Commonwealth on education matters relating to Indigenous peoples, histories and cultures.

We meet twice a term at a different school within our region each time, and tonight we are finally meeting in my old primary school. I have been waiting for this occasion, to return physically as an adult to a place where so much of my energy and growth has lived.

I stand here as a fully grown person and my energy speaks to my child-self. We are both here – now and then – simultaneously.

I feel it in my cells just as I feel my presence amongst these bookshelves that I once scoured for books on white tigers.

This place has barely changed at all. The colours and scents are how I remember them. There on the library wall where we are meeting is the large honour board showing my name, and that I was awarded dux of the school when I graduated in year six.

But out the window the view has changed significantly. Though the trains still rumble past, the lead smelter is gone, having closed when I was in high school. In its place there now stands a mammoth Bunnings and Costco. Proximity to that site out the window no longer means lead poisoning, just easily accessible and affordable school snacks and an abundance of indoor plants waiting for me to impulse buy them.

Kicking up pebbles as I walk along the street, it is not yet 8:30 am but the sun already has bite. The journey to school feels like it takes a lifetime and it's even worse when the weather is too hot, cold or wet. Our house is on the same street as the school – at the opposite end – but that street runs the length of the entire suburb, so it is not a short walk.

The sun beats down. I do not own a hat. With holes in my sneakers I am glad for the heat instead of the wet; having wet socks is both an irritation and embarrassment that I know from experience disrupts my concentration at school.

Kick, kick, squint.

The pattern of my walking is punctuated only by the low rumble of trains travelling out of sight along the track, which runs behind the line of houses to my left. The magpies warble from their tree at the top of the hill that marks the halfway point between home and school. Sometimes if neighbourhood kids are walking with me, the magpies will swoop them, but they never swoop me. I am their friend, and today I walk alone.

I carry my school bag on my back but there is no lunchbox, drink bottle or hat inside of it, just some crumpled paper. I carry it purely for aesthetics: you are *supposed* to have your bag, and by carrying mine people will assume I have the items that are also meant to be within it. It is less embarrassing this way.

Crap! Just over halfway to school and I realise I have forgotten my homework book. I don't have a watch but it's a safe bet that I do not have time to turn around now, and I know I don't have the energy. I continue on without it.

Walking through the school gates, I find and play with my friends until the morning bell rings. I am nine years old. My older sister now goes to high school and, having moved from Sydney to Lake Macquarie last year, I am still adjusting to the sensory overload of this new school. The trains that run along the tracks are fully visible if you are up on the school field, and their scheduled appearances make the school buildings shake.

The first time a train went past while I was seated cross-legged on the carpeted classroom floor, the sensation of the building rocking and the sound of the rattling had me thinking there was an earthquake. I screeched with fear and the kids all laughed as the teacher explained it was just the trains and that after a while I would stop noticing it.

As well as a train line, there is also a large smelter that looms up into the sky in full sight of our classrooms. All day a steamy, smoky substance of some sort pours forth from the large towers. I am convinced it is that stuff that makes the air here smell funny but the other kids insist the smell is all in my head.

If the sounds and scents are a lot to get used to, they are nothing compared to the shock of learning that every year the entire student body is subject to in-school blood tests. It seems like a normal school day, and then nurses will arrive and set up to conduct blood tests in the school library. An annual and compulsory ritual undertaken to measure the level of lead that is held in our young bodies; lead that permeates the air and the soil here, courtesy of that smelter.

No child enjoys needles, but as the child of intravenous drug users, the sight of orange caps and syringes now causes me to break out in cold sweats. No matter, no mind, no exceptions – every kid has to be bled in order to monitor our lead levels – so along with everyone else I have to go through the process of having blood taken. It adds to the things making it harder to like it here. I miss my old school, my grandparents' house on Dharug Country, and I *really* miss my grandparents, even though Pop tries to visit as often as he can.

Dad is increasingly absent, Mum has been unravelling; it is isolating and I feel lonely. Pop drives up to stay whenever he can afford to. Sometimes he stays here at our home. Sometimes he takes us kids and we stay together at a motel near the beach, sometimes further north, and sometimes just close by here on Awabakal Country, but wherever we go, there's always fishing and strawberry milkshakes. We don't get to travel to Yuin Country anymore; with Great-Grandma Lucy having passed away that home is now a place of belonging to a new family.

When Pop arrives, we get in the car and disappear for hours and hours to the local beaches where we enjoy the surf, explore caves and swim. Just us kids, Pop, and moments of rest from an increasingly tumultuous home.

13

'THAT'S ONE THING WE GOT right – our kids always told us everything.'

Mum is doing that thing again where she talks about me like I'm not in the room. I am not convinced she is aware that I *am* in the room, if I am honest. I look over at her – she isn't seeing me.

'If anyone ever approached our kids, or tried any funny business, our kids would have told us. We got that right.' Mum's thumb is digging into her own chest dramatically as she talks, watching the report on the news about sexual assault of children.

My anger begins to bubble up.

'We got a lot wrong but our kids never experienced that, thank Christ.'

To be fair to Mum, she believes what she's saying, and she has good reason to because I have never once disclosed to her.

Growing up we were taught the power of words; the power of language. If you said you saw *the exact same item but in a different colour,* Mum couldn't let it go. *That's not exact, Amy, that's similar,* she would correct. I was an avid talker who devoured books with the same voraciousness as Mum – while many were surprised I made it to university, no-one was surprised to hear I majored in English literature when I did.

So a talker who didn't tell? Unfathomable to Mum.

But as kids our home was often a site of overwhelm. You can't disclose or report to someone who is only semi-conscious, and you learn to pick your battles to avoid rocking the boat or disrupting moods. The threat wasn't inside the house. I just chose to never tell. But tonight … tonight I feel like telling.

'Mum, I am one of those kids, part of those stats.'

She turns to face me, her eyes narrow, seeing me now.

'What do you mean? You were abused as a kid, were you? Bullshit!'

I am shocked by her response; it stuns me to silence.

'That's what I thought.' She smirks, turning back to the television.

My anger is simmering. 'Well, I was, so …'

Mum jumps to her feet, eyes wide, yelling now. 'You would have told me! Abused by whom?'

'Mum, sit down.'

My anger dissipates and I start crying. I loathe crying but through tears I tell her it wasn't our family and it was no-one in our home. But there was a neighbour who used to take me into their garden shed and lock the door, and a sitter who used to hurt me when I was left with them when I was really young, too young to even have all the words I would have needed to disclose then.

Mum listens quietly but she looks terrified, disgusted, distressed. Her face is glitching, twitching – she can't seem to settle on an emotion. What is the main one? Horror?

Finally she sits down and making a 'W' sign with her hands, she mutters, 'Whatever.'

Whatever? Whatever I was expecting it wasn't that.

'What do you mean *whatever?* That's not a reasonable response, Mum. Jesus Christ!'

She settles on rage as her emotion now but her eyes leak as she screams, 'WHY ARE YOU TELLING ME NOW? WHAT DO YOU WANT ME TO DO ABOUT IT TWENTY YEARS LATER?'

There's nothing she could do now. She's right, but her words sting. I go quiet and she turns back to the television and changes the channel. I regret saying anything.

The school day done – a storm has been brewing and lightning dances across the sky as I walk out of the school gates and back down the street towards home. The clouds break and the rain begins to soak me through, just as I begin to descend down the hill where the magpies nest. Halfway home.

I am annoyed that Mum hasn't bothered to come and pick me up; the storm was building all afternoon, and I am sure she is just sitting at home. I hate walking in the rain. In my frustration I am kicking gravel through puddles, accepting that my shoes and socks will be drenched soon anyway, when a car drives up beside me.

There is a man in the driver's seat. His car is facing the same direction that I am walking – he has pulled up in the gutter, right next to where I am walking. He is on the wrong side of the road.

I stop from the shock of the car's arrival so close to me, and I step off the road and up onto the wet grass. The man motions that he wants to talk. He winds down the window. I wonder if he is lost.

'You shouldn't be walking alone in the rain,' he says.

His tone sounds friendly but my tummy says this feels fake.

'I'm fine,' I say, and begin to walk again. Something is off about this.

He allows his car to roll along beside me as I walk on the grass verge. He continues to talk to me through the window; his car still on the wrong side of the otherwise empty road.

'How far away is your home? I will give you a lift.'

I say nothing.

'Get in.'

'No, I am almost home,' I lie, knowing I am still several bends in the road away from our house.

'I am going in the same direction as you. Just get in the car.'

His voice sounds less friendly now; it has an edge to it – he seems to be getting angry. I suspect we both know this road is a dead end but I doubt he knows which house is mine.

'My house is just down here,' I lie again, and point a few doors ahead to the only house that has a car visible in its driveway.

'GET IN THE CAR!' He pumps the brakes, opens the passenger door and is yelling at me.

It begins to absolutely bucket down with rain. I leg it, sprinting for the house I had pointed to, praying that someone will be home, and that someone will be kind.

As soon as my feet hit the driveway, the man slams his passenger door shut and does a 180-turn at speed. The car's engine audibly revs as he drives off over the hill in the opposite direction to where I am heading, of where he claimed to be going.

I run up the driveway and stand on the small verandah of the housing commission home I had claimed was my own. I am too scared to knock but also scared the man will come back. I know I am still fifteen minutes walking distance from my own house. I don't know what to do.

I stand there, soaked through, shaken but unable to move. I might only be nine but I recognise that I am stuck between two potentially dangerous positions. Do I knock, or should I leg it once more and run as fast as I can home?

I decide to make a run for it, almost slipping as I leap from the verandah of this randomly picked house. I don't stop running until I get home, and the car doesn't appear again.

I burst through my front door, panting and shaking.

Before I can say anything, Mum is yelling at me for dripping water in the house.

I ignore her and yell back, 'Mum, it is storming! Why didn't you come and pick me up?'

'Don't be so dramatic, go and get dry, Amy.'

Mum is in a mood. So I add this story to the long list of moments I never share with her. I throw my always-empty backpack in the bathroom where the drips won't matter, and don't bother trying to tell Mum about the man in the car. I strip off and put my shoes upside down on top of the washing machine.

Hopefully the weather and my shoes will be dry in time for walking to school in the morning.

14

RIVING TO SCHOOL PICK-UP, MUSIC up loud, afternoon sun glinting across the lake, I sing along to beautiful lyrics about childhood rooms being packed into boxes. I am on my way to collect my own children from their school, and reflect that my own childhood can be packed into no box – as it lived in no room – it lived and lives within my body. I carry it within my cells, and it was passed on within the creation of my own children. I am of them, and they are of me. Just as I am of my siblings and parents and ancestors. We are, together.

Mrs Smith enters the school kitchens and, ignoring the loud chatter of a full class, walks directly to the class roll, which is on the front desk. Week one of high school and I am pumped for cooking class. Dad never got the opportunity to finish high school but when he was there, he'd loved Design and Technology, especially cooking. He considered it quite genius of him and his best mate to choose what was back then a female-dominated elective. He learnt to cook and from the way he told it – and he often did tell it – he did very well with the young women in those classes too.

Mrs Smith is an older woman with short curly hair as white as the flour that sits in tubs on the benches in front of us. She is quietly reading out the roll while the class all talk to their neighbours. We've come from a variety of primary schools so I only know one other child in this class, and as one of the youngest in the year, I have only just turned twelve.

'AMY TEERMAN!'

My name rings out of the teacher's mouth, immediately stunning me into silence.

'Amy? Stand up!'

She is glancing around the room and I realise she doesn't know which prepubescent student belongs to the name she is speaking. I am tempted to just stay seated but don't want to get in trouble my very first week.

I stand, tentative.

'Amy Teerman?' she repeats, eyes narrowing on me.

I am at the very back table in the room. Her voice carries easily across, as the whole class turn their faces to look at me.

I nod.

'Do you have an older sister named Lisa?'

I pause before answering. Lisa and I are very different when it comes to school – she gets in trouble a lot.

'Yes, Lisa is my sister,' I answer reluctantly.

I glance around the room. I am nervous and don't want to make eye contact with this woman who looks like Mrs Claus but is giving off definite Grinch vibes.

'Amy, you are *nothing*. Your whole family are *nothing*, and you will always be nothing. Just like them.'

Her statement, and the cold confidence with which she delivers it causes my eyes to pivot back to her in disbelief. I stare at her in silence. I can feel the stares of my fellow students on me.

'Get out!' She states it firmly, decisively.

'What?'

'Get out of my classroom, you aren't welcome here.'

I don't move, sure there must be an error. I'm also just deeply confused about where I am even supposed to go. I look at the other people at my table; some are looking at me also clearly unsure what is happening, but others are looking down. They're embarrassed for me, for what she has said about my family.

I shift in my cheap shoes, and when it becomes clear that she isn't going to start the class while I am there, I gather my notebook and pens and I leave. I am still packing my bag out in the corridor when I hear her in a considerably altered tone welcome the class warmly and begin the lesson.

I sling my bag over my shoulder and walk to the toilet

block. The smell of smoking wafts out and doors slam shut as I enter – students mistaking me for a teacher. I pick a cubicle in the farthest corner, and locking the door I sit there until the bell rings for next period.

For the rest of the year, almost every time I attempt to enter the cooking classrooms, I am instructed to leave. On the few occasions this doesn't occur, Mrs Smith loudly critiques my attempts at cooking, which were always going to be pretty terrible. In light of the anxiety I feel in her presence, my attempts are absolutely appalling; I can't even boil noodles in that room without something going wrong, and every time it does go wrong, her eagle eyes are quick to spot it.

It isn't just cooking class where Lisa's reputation precedes me. The music teacher, Mrs Carry, seems to also hate me on sight. Though not as direct and open in the first instance as Mrs Smith, she makes it abundantly clear that when it comes to anything music related, I am the embodiment of failure.

It is only in science class where being Lisa's sister somehow works in my favour; for reasons unknown to me, Lisa not only behaved but was charming for that teacher. I sit up the front in science class, learning about Bunsen burners under her smiling and instructive teaching.

Around halfway through that first year in high school – as I begin to adjust to the way our schedule works, moving between classrooms and engaging in various subjects – I start to realise there is a mainstream cohort but there is also a segregated class called 'Emerald'. Emerald is for the *smart kids*. Rumour has it they get the better textbooks and better teachers as well as smaller class sizes. To enter Emerald in year seven, you had to sit an exam in year six. I hadn't even heard of the exam, let alone attempted to sit it.

I know I am good at a lot of school, and wonder if I should be in with the other nerds instead of in my class where people throw hands a lot. I don't mind that the kids fight – I can hold my own and I do – but it makes it hard to learn new content when the teacher spends so much time trying to corral the class. In third term, one of the boys chucks a stool at our math teacher, and that teacher responds by walking out and isn't seen again for six weeks. Stress leave.

English is my favourite class. The teacher, Mr Bernard, is a big believer in extrinsic motivation. At the end of each class he asks a difficult question; it is always related to that day's content. The student who is called on and can answer correctly gets to visit him in the staffroom at recess to collect their reward – a cold can of Coke from a stash he keeps in a dedicated bar fridge. I am highly food and reward motivated, so I listen intently, and score the can of Coke several times a week.

I struggle with Personal Development, and Health and Physical Education the most. In a time before trigger warnings, I sit through various classes labelled 'drug education' that seem to just demonise anyone who struggles with addiction. Worse than the way drug addiction itself is portrayed, though, are the side remarks often made by the class teacher – disparaging and dehumanising.

He shows us graphs but adds his own commentary; making statements such as, 'All children of junkies become junkies. It isn't a nice thing to say but it's accurate.'

I sit and I fume as he makes these comments but I don't dare challenge him. He often makes remarks about the children of drug addicts, emphasising that they sometimes have birth defects and abnormalities, and that you can pretty much spot them on sight.

People can spot me on sight? I don't think that's accurate but I am terrified he will announce to the class that I am one of the children he is talking about. The only thing I learnt in that class was that high school wasn't a place of safe adults who I might talk to – or ask questions of – when it came to what I was experiencing at home.

As luck or perhaps misfortune would have it, in the final week of the school year – when the grades from the end-of-year exams are released – I am in music class when the year-level adviser, Mrs Sparks, comes looking for me. Knocking on the door she calls me out to the hallway for a private conversation. I have no idea what is going on; the adviser hasn't noticed me all year, so why is she pulling me out of class? Whatever it is, the music teacher, Mrs Carry, isn't having any of it, and follows us into the hall with the energy of an angry bulldog.

I am not sure if I am in trouble, if there is a home emergency, or something else; so I am tentative and bracing myself but Mrs Sparks is all smiles.

'Amy! You dark horse!'

I stare, confused.

'You are not going to believe this but you have come first in the entire year for English. Your marks are up there in pretty much every subject!'

I love school, and found the exams easy. So I have no trouble believing it, but the fact she does tells me a lot.

'A note will be sent home today but these grades mean you have to transition to Emerald next year when school returns. I wanted to tell you personally and congratulate you.'

I thank Mrs Sparks and as she moves away Mrs Carry, who is smiling with her mouth but not her eyes, tells me to wait in the hall with her for a moment.

We stand there awkwardly waiting for Mrs Sparks to round the corner and once the sound of her footsteps fade away, Mrs Carry drops the false smile. Planting her finger squarely into my chest she pushes me; I step back until I am up against the brick wall.

Her finger still firmly pressing into me, she breathes into my face.

'You do not belong in Emerald. Do you know how that class works, Amy?'

I am a mixture of kinda frightened, kinda enraged by this strange woman but answer honestly.

'No, I don't.'

'If you get in, someone has to leave. You do not deserve to be there. Those other students – they do. I am going to fight this. I am not allowing it.'

Dropping her finger, she doesn't wait for a response, just turns and re-enters her class. I follow and take my seat and she acts like nothing has happened, continuing with our lesson as before Mrs Sparks arrived.

For the rest of that day every teacher who passes me in the hall attempts a high-five or gives me an excited, 'Well done!' Several of them make comments along the lines of, 'Look out, here comes the dark horse!'

I *love* school, I am *good* at school. The fact these adults all seem so thoroughly surprised that my marks are good shocks me. I may only be twelve, but between the teachers who dislike me, such as Mrs Smith and Mrs Carry, and the general air of surprise from the teachers only now noticing me, it feels as though they all think I have somehow magicked my way into good grades. I begin to realise that nobody here can see me outside of being a member of a poor, not very good family.

When I get home that afternoon Mum and Dad are both there and already know. The school rang them and they're elated. Dad is on the phone to my grandparents when I walk in – everyone is sending their congratulations.

Later that night, Dad mentions quietly that he had actually assumed I would already be in the smart class, and I explain we must have missed the intake last year. Mum is on the couch reading but glances up, smiling. 'No matter, Lou. You're there now, where you belong.'

15

WHEN I AM GOING ABOUT the work of adulthood, the world often seems too loud; the overwhelm tempting me to seek means to drown it out to avoid complete burnout. When I head back to home Country, ancestral Country, even with the squeals and chatter of the children and yinarr (women) around the fire, the volume drops to a whisper and the constant binding of my chest that accompanies my ever-present anxiety begins to loosen.

'All these gaayili (children) making me clucky, aunties,' I say as I stir the coffee.

To my surprise the Elders *tsk* at me. 'Nahhh, baby bird, no more babies for you. Don't even speak that way here where spirits will hear you.'

I laugh and shake my head in dissent. 'Surely I have more babies in me,' I say, patting my belly.

But again, they do not agree with me. 'Time for you to

rest, bub, no more nappies and ...' Aunt touches her chest to indicate breastfeeding and we all laugh.

'I got barely any left from my first two, ay.' I tap my chest too.

The conversation moves on as the dragonflies dip in and out of camp and one of the men adds wood to the fire.

I fall to sleep easily that night; no insomnia here on Grandmother Country.

The sun is setting as I rummage through the piles of discarded laundry, checking pockets and shaking jeans in the hope of finding coins. Continuing on to the kitchen, I look behind stacks of books, plates and knick-knacks that sit cluttered on benchtops. Lifting, moving and sticking my hand into any spaces where a coin might fall and go unnoticed.

In the living room I move quietly. Mum is on one couch in the corner and appears to be asleep. I get in behind the other couch's pillows and shift stacks of papers and more books that sit along the wall. It is getting dark inside and I kick something, knocking over a bong that is on the floor between the two couches. There is a *clunk* and splash as the bong tips – water spilling over the floorboards.

I dry heave from the horrific smell. Mum's lack of movement at the sounds makes me realise she isn't asleep after all – she is on the nod. I can put the light on and search with gusto now, knowing she won't wake regardless of how much noise I make.

My efforts are rewarded with a total of $4 in coins; two gold coins and a handful of silver. I lift the bong back to standing position and throw a dirty towel on the puddle where the water spilt. Flicking off the light I sprint out the front door, my pocket jingling as I head towards the local shopping centre on foot.

I have started dancing at school. We meet at lunchtimes and will be part of a regional performance called Star-Struck. Star-Struck is a dance festival that many schools take part in annually, and is so well loved it even airs on television. We have been practising for weeks. It doesn't *technically* cost anything to join the dance groups in school. But I have had to scrounge for coins to get the buses to the rehearsals, and all the dancing has made me even hungrier, which is hard when we often have nothing in the cupboards.

We require costumes for the festival, and most of the dancers go to costume makers with their parents but that is something I could never afford. Someone lets me know that we might be able to access fabric from the Design and Technology classroom closet. After promising the fabric gatekeeper that I would, of course, pay the 'voluntary' school fees as soon as possible to cover the supplies, I am able to raid the stock to find something close to what we have been told to source. I am never going to be able to pay those fees, no matter how many times the office calls our home landline.

A mum of a neighbourhood kid I am friends with is handy with a sewing machine, and has offered to make the costume for me if I get her the fabric and design instructions, which I do. After reading the note I bring from school, she points out I am also supposed to have a particular coloured pair of shoes. I only own one pair of shoes and we agree I can't afford to buy more.

She helps me problem-solve and comes up with the idea of making a pair of fabric socks to cover my existing shoes. We are all wearing different colours, and my assigned colour is a beautiful royal blue. When I bring my shoe covers with me to the next rehearsal, the dance teacher pulls a face but doesn't comment.

Several afternoons in the lead-up to the festival we come together to practise with students from other schools. It is hard work learning the choreography and dancing along with students from schools all around the region, and I have no food beyond an apple most days. I drink as much water as possible, and in breaks go searching for a free tea and coffee station.

I am only fourteen but I am already a seasoned coffee drinker – sometimes instant coffee is the only thing in the house. And I know that if I find a drink station, I can make myself a free sugary cup of tea or coffee to help stop the head spins I have from hunger. If I find one, I am always relieved when it is out of the way so that the other students won't see me using it.

I am doing partnered dancing for one of the dances. I will be lifted and spun in the air as part of the routine. It is glorious, but hardly the princess–prince situation I would have liked.

My dance partner keeps making comments to me that I don't quite understand, but am pretty sure are sexual in nature. We are all around the same ages but clearly in different phases of puberty. I have no interest at all in flirting; so when we aren't actively rehearsing I retreat to be with the other girls and whatever supervising teacher we have that day.

As we draw closer to the performance itself, the teachers instruct us to pack hearty lunches and plenty of snacks, as there are day and night-time shows, and we won't be going anywhere in between. There is no food at home in the cupboard. I also know I am due for my period, meaning I will need to buy sanitary items if I can't find enough at home, which I can't. So I resort to searching the house for any coins I can find.

And that's how – the night before Star-Struck commences – I come to be in Woolworths with $4 in my pocket, and the smell of bong water wafting up from my shoes. I walk up and down each and every aisle, finding the cheapest tampons on the shelf – they're $3.20 – and then attempting to find a food that I can spread out over three days that will cost eighty cents or less. Security follow me up and down the aisles, as they always do. Staff members who know my family will also hover. They always hover, but never help. I ignore them, focusing on math.

Bread costs $1 – that's too much. I could get one bread roll but that can't be divided across the days. In the confectionery aisle I see a single packet of plain chips is an option but it's very small and the other kids will likely notice if I keep eating from the same packet each day. I eventually discover that a four pack of Homebrand powdered chicken noodle soups costs eighty-four cents. I jingle the coins in my hand, examining the mix of five-cent pieces, and wonder if maybe the cashier won't realise that I am short five cents.

I stand there considering whether I will get away with it if I try to buy the soup and the tampons. Or will they ask me for the extra coin and I will be left shamed at the checkout when I can't produce it and am denied the two items I need. I walk back to the sanitary aisle and see that the tampons are actually $3.15 not $3.20, which means I have exactly the right amount. I purchase the tampons and powdered soup and after security check my bag, I walk home hoping there will be some bread at home that I might take for dipping.

Once back, I see there's no bread and the fridge is empty of butter and milk. Fuck. I sit at the table and complete my homework, knowing I have to drop it into school in the morning before the bus leaves for dancing.

I rise early in the morning but clearly not earlier than Dad. I stand in the kitchen and can feel that he has already been in here this morning. There is half a loaf of fresh bread sitting on the bench. *Yay!* There is no cling wrap but I find butter in the fridge. *Hurrah!* So I butter some slices and wrap them in newspaper before placing the bundle at the bottom of my backpack. I then pack a mug, my four packets of powdered soup, the tampons, dance costume, and an empty cordial bottle I find in the recycling bin to use for drinking water.

Mum is still in bed. Taylah and Max are watching cartoons in the living room and Dad has already left for work. His empty coffee mug sits on the dining table, acting as a paperweight on a handwritten note he has left me on the kitchen table.

Good morning Lou,

If you don't stand for something, you may well fall for anything.

xoxo Dad

The base of the cup has left a coffee-coloured semi-circle crossing the corner of the scrap of paper, looking like a rising sun. I pop the note in my pocket and head out in the early morning light to start the two-kilometre walk to school.

The energy of the dance festival is electric. We sit around on our school bags, some kids have brought camp chairs, others towels, and we spread out in our little makeshift waiting bays. I make a note to myself to bring a towel to sit on tomorrow. The supervising teacher is seated in a large camp chair, as she reads a glossy magazine and makes comments about the models within it: 'Look at her legs, they go all the way to her arse.' I don't really understand what that means. I subtly run my hand up my own thighs – my legs also go to my arse. Does the teacher have an additional joint? What am I missing?

Eventually I realise I am interpreting her commentary too literally. She is actually just praising the model for being slim. The other girls look over the teacher's shoulder as they munch on their packed lunches and comment about their loathed cellulite. I don't know what cellulite is, and find their discussions confusing if I am totally honest, but I am so happy to be here. I sit and think about my steps and moves, anxious I will misstep.

We spend three days and evenings together. On the second night, when other kids have pizza orders being delivered courtesy of their parents, a teacher spotting me with just my cup of soup, loudly remarks, 'Is that all you packed to eat, Amy?' These kinds of comments draw attention to me but are never accompanied with an offer of support. It is frustrating and embarrassing, but I suspect both the teacher and the other girls I sit with just assume I am intentionally not eating much.

On the third day when my stomach rumbles in a quiet moment, one of the girls sitting close by casually comments that she really doesn't want her bread roll. She hands it to me without fuss, saying, 'Amy, don't let me waste it, eat it for me.'

I feel like she knows but I deeply appreciate the way she makes it seem as though I am the one doing her a favour. I try to look unphased as I eat the roll but it means a lot to me in that moment because I am starving hungry.

The days and evenings at Star-Struck are long. But it feels

phenomenal to be performing in front of crowds of people, and the way my costume moves feels nothing short of magical.

When the festival finishes, parents flood the foyer, and some bring flowers for their dancer daughters. My parents aren't there, and I don't receive flowers, but I didn't miss a step on stage and that knowledge is elating.

I get a lift home with one of the other girls. I jump out of the car with a 'Thanks!' and scurry down the front path, hoping there will be something to eat in the kitchen. Walking in the door I realise it must be payday because Dad has ordered Chinese food and everyone is in the kitchen, clearly in a great mood.

'There she is! Our tiny dancer!' Dad exclaims when he sees me.

Mum smiles at me, passing me a plate. We all sit together at the dining table, and after I wolf down my rice and lemon chicken, Mum requests that I put my dance costume back on and show them some of the moves I learnt.

'Sorry we couldn't come see you dance, Lou. The tickets were real expensive,' Dad mumbles, as he scoops more beef and black bean onto his plate.

I run to go wash my face, pull my dance costume back on and return to the kitchen with a flourish, twirling for my family before bedtime. We don't have the song, so I sing it as I move through the steps. They all clap loudly when I finish and I take a bow.

It's been a good week.

16

THE WIND WHIPS THROUGH MY hair, the waves crash, the salt is visible in the air. La Nina has made a mess of the summer but it's delightfully refreshing and the wind means people aren't trying to talk to me as I sit here, headphones on, iced coffee in hand. The wind knocks the coffee over; the beige wet sprays over a curious bird who was sitting close. I save the drink but place it now between my feet, so my hands can rest.

Come June this seat will give me views of the whales as they migrate. Dolphins will play around them; their forms cascading as surfers sit still on their boards respectfully watching and waiting their turn.

I've heard people say that nature knows best: that animals don't rush or stress or worry. They just *are*. But I suspect people who talk like that understand little about what they call the natural world. I watched a documentary once on orcas; they kill and torment other creatures for fun. The film showed orcas chasing this whale and her calf for days and days, for as long as it took to exhaust the mother whale so she could no longer protect her baby. They killed the calf. Not to eat, just because. Then they swam away, leaving the mother with her now-dead baby. And she visibly mourned that baby for days. Even when she eventually swam away, I don't believe she let that moment go. It's white-people nonsense to say that nature doesn't grieve and mourn, that nature isn't cruel. We are no less nature than those whales and orcas.

Sometimes I can't tell if my mother is orca or whale. When I was a child and she was enraged, I felt like the mother whale – under attack for days and trying desperately to just escape. But as an adult when she is angry I see her as the mother whale, and her demons and unmet needs are the orcas, attacking her and breaking her down relentlessly, until she's left with nothing except the task to grieve. And she doesn't grieve. She erases. Ignores. Throws out the comment, *It's only a big deal if you make it one.*

The lesson is clear: we are never to make it one.

We argue in my adulthood about my childhood. Sometimes she forgets I'm in the room and tells someone a story about when we were kids that is so blatantly false, I find myself becoming the orca. I bubble over and verbally attack her; I use my words against her, again and again. She fights back, tone gentler than mine, but her words are denials and they sting.

And even while I'm doing it, I recognise from decades of the same pattern that there is no resolution. Though I am a fully grown adult, with my own family, home, life and power, it is my child-self that is emerging to attack her when we fight. She won't admit I'm right, and we can't go back and undo what has been done. Yet I attack anyway. I'm the orca chasing her down emotionally in those moments, even though I've no intention of consuming what I tear off.

For years I have been counting down to turning fourteen years and nine months old – eager to take a job and begin working at McDonalds as soon as I am legally able. I've been working unofficially at other retail and hospitality places since I turned twelve. But those bosses often took advantage of the fact I couldn't legally be on the books, underpaying me and sometimes not paying me at all. I feel disempowered in so many parts of my life; but hitting puberty when you live in poverty with erratic and unpredictable parents is its own special kind of waking nightmare.

There are times when there is no money for sanitary items, and I resort to cutting up towels to use as pads. This is particularly anxiety-inducing when it happens on school days, and while I won't know it until I am in my thirties, I have endometriosis, which will grow throughout my bowels and around my uterus in adulthood. Heavy bleeding and extreme pain, especially when you have little or no access to pads, tampons, heat packs and painkillers, make hard days even harder.

I also don't own a complete school uniform, and this is problematic when an incorrect uniform is treated as a punishable offence. I hate how often I am punished for things completely outside of my control. I know I have no choice but to work as much as possible – I need to be able to provide for myself financially so I can meet these basic needs and better focus at school. I am determined to go to university, but I am repeatedly told that this requires exceptionally high grades. Though I am often internally overwhelmed, I am also entrepreneurial and scrappy, always looking for opportunities to make ends meet. While I'm not treated as one of the 'pretty girls' at school, I am often told by adults that I have the height, face and hair for modelling and acting. So I keep an eye out for any of those kinds of opportunities, in the hope of making some money.

As fate and timing will have it, the same week that I can finally go for my McDonalds interview, I also go for my first acting audition. I had asked my parents and with their permission planned for the trip. Mum was supposed to take me, but on the day she is in a terrible mood and doesn't get out of bed. I am too scared to travel so far by myself and I have no money; but thankfully Lisa steps in, finding some coins hidden in one of Mum's drawers, and she agrees to accompany me.

On a sunny day in spring Lisa and I leave home to catch a bus, a train, and two more buses so I can audition for a feature role in KFC's upcoming Christmas commercial. On the train, for the two hours it takes to get down into the city, Lisa brushes and braids my hair.

We have never been to this part of Sydney before, and with limited resources and no map, we inevitably get lost, catching the wrong bus, and having to walk for several blocks. I arrive at the audition an hour late and perspiring. But I am dressed neatly with two braids in my hair and am told they will make an exception; I will still be permitted to audition.

I sit with empty hands in a lobby with several stunningly beautiful girls, each holding professional photographs and printed résumés. My mouth is dry from the hot walk and panic of being late. I feel like an imposter next to these polished girls, and am worried that my poverty and inexperience is carried on me like a stench, which in hindsight it may well have been. But when I finally get called in, the audition is actually really fun; the adults are kind and friendly as I join them in a large, quiet and air conditioned room.

They don't seem bothered when I explain that I have no photographs or documents to give them. They nod along as I speak and then instruct me to talk about my favourite part of school, and to *not hold back*. I begin to explain how I love creative arts, and how enjoyable it is to take clay and shape the materials in my hands, until I am eventually looking at a pot or vase or some kind of vessel that I can call my own. I move my hands as I talk, and noting their encouraging cues, I give more details and speak enthusiastically. When I am done they smile, thank me for coming, and let me know they will be in touch.

Lisa and I leave, and getting on the correct bus this time, head back to the train and arrive home within a few hours.

At dinner Dad asks me about the audition, and I explain that Lisa took me. He shoots a dirty glance at Mum. She avoids his gaze but isn't apologetic.

A few weeks later, during my first shift at the local McDonalds, my dad calls the store and lets me know that my audition was successful; I will feature in this year's KFC Christmas commercial. He is proud of me and says I have to let my boss know that I will need a day off soon in order to go and film. My manager is really happy for me, saying that won't be a problem, and I am ecstatic.

For being in the commercial I will be paid $2000 for the one day! I plan to use my money to get new school shoes, runners, and a complete uniform.

When I get home from work that night Mum is clearly excited about the news of my successful audition. She has cut some carrots and celery for me, and pushes the bowl in front of me, explaining that girls who go on television need to 'eat well'. As we will be filming from early in the morning, Mum books a cheap hotel for the night before filming, so we can travel down the day before.

When the day arrives, instead of getting ready for school, I pack an overnight bag, and Mum and I head to the train station. One bus and two trains later we arrive at a small hotel near a strip of shops. We will film tomorrow at a house that production have booked. I am so nervous and excited that I can hardly sleep. Mum's mood is low and she leaves me alone in the hotel for a while that night but she returns before I am asleep. In the morning everything goes smoothly. We arrive on set together and on time.

I have so much fun filming the commercial – I think I could do this forever. I get to bite into freshly made KFC all day long; everyone is friendly and happy to answer the numerous questions I ask about how things work. The director talks me through the way all of the details, even the colours of the clothing I have been dressed in, are chosen with intention. There is yummy catering for lunch, and when we wrap, I am tired but really proud of myself.

It is only that evening on the way home that things go wrong. Mum's behaviour becomes increasingly erratic as we head to the first train station. She is walking so fast I struggle to keep up with her, and whenever I speak to her, she ignores me. Getting on the train I sit beside her, only to have her get up and leave the carriage. Initially I think she's just seeking out the train toilet, so I stay seated and wait. But she doesn't return, and some time later, as the train pulls into Hornsby Station, I spot her through the window as she exits the train and heads quickly down the platform.

I grab my bag and leg it out of the carriage before it departs with me inside. I give chase and catch up to her on the next platform over. She scowls at me but says nothing. I stand a few metres back and watch her, incredibly confused.

When a train arrives and she gets aboard, I follow her on. When she sits, I sit beside her. She responds to this by getting up again and leaving the carriage. But this time I don't wait. I follow her. She takes a seat, I again sit beside her, she again gets up and moves carriages.

We repeat this pattern three or four times before I work out that this train is definitely heading to Newcastle. We will be on it for a while so I give up trying to sit next to her and find a seat a few rows down but in the same carriage. She stays seated and, closing her eyes, appears to go to sleep. I am tired but am not willing to risk closing my eyes.

Almost two hours later the train pulls into Cardiff Station and I watch Mum swiftly get up and exit the train without so much as a glance in my direction. She still hasn't spoken to me since we left the set. I disembark and follow her at a distance as she walks out of the station and down the main road. It is dark now and getting late – it has been a long day. Mum comes to a bus stop and begins to read the timetable. I wonder if she is just pretending to read so that I can catch up with her, so I approach.

Assuming we will be waiting together for a bus, which I am confident I will hear arrive, I place my bag down on the bus stop bench and turn to look in the shop window behind us. The window is filled with beautiful skirts and dresses. I allow myself a moment of indulgence and think to myself that maybe I will buy myself one when I get the money from today. Two thousand dollars is, after all, more than enough for the school uniform I need.

It can't have been more than a minute or so before I turn back around and find that both Mum and my bag are gone. I look up and down the street but can't see her. I am not sure what to do, so I sit on the cold metal bus seat and wait. I have no phone, no jacket, my wallet is in my bag, and I don't know where Mum has gone. I have never tried to walk home from here, except along the train tracks themselves, but I know I am several kilometres from our house. My guess is it would take me maybe an hour to walk along the roads, and I am scared to attempt it alone this late at night.

So I sit for a while in the spot where I had placed my now-missing bag, and wait in the quiet hoping Mum will reappear. It is mid-week, the shops are closed – the only noises are coming from the pub and Chinese restaurant up the hill. I can see my breath in front of me as I wait, and don't know how long I sit there before it occurs to me that Mum probably isn't coming back. If a bus arrives I actually have no money with me to be able to get on. I have no choice but to try to walk home alone.

I walk, and I walk, and after a while I start to cry. I don't know what the time is.

Over an hour of walking, when I eventually walk in the front door at home Dad is sitting at the table, coffee in front of him, looking very worried.

'Amy! Where have you been? Your mother has been home for two hours!'

I cry and explain that Mum left me at the bus stop and took my bag. He tells me Mum arrived home in a taxi and has been refusing to say where I was, and that my bag is on the kitchen bench.

She never explains why she did it. But a few weeks later, when the production company deposit the pay for my day of filming, I discover my parents gave their bank account details, not mine. They keep all of the money. I am enraged but have no power. I never see a cent of that payment and I never audition for another television commercial.

17

THROUGHOUT HIGH SCHOOL MUM'S MENTAL health had rapidly deteriorated; her behaviour becoming increasingly unpredictable. By year eight I had developed the habit of leaving school early each day, so as to get home and deal with whatever Taylah and Max – then only nine and seven – might otherwise find when they return from school. I couldn't exactly tell the office that I was concerned my mum might be starting fires, or passed out naked in the house; so I would make some excuse to leave the classroom, usually claiming I needed the restroom, and then I would slip out the school gate with the aim of getting home before Taylah and Max.

If I could get there first and Mum was in a state, I would be able to smooth it over; cover her with a blanket, move items away that children shouldn't see. Hopefully do enough so that they wouldn't be conscious of what was happening.

Early on in year ten, I am pacing through the summer air, walking the two kilometres home from school. It is February and as I walk I worry about the fact that I am supposed to be going to live with Dad for a while. If I am up in Kempsey with Dad, there will be no-one to watch out for Tay and Max. Dad has been away for a few months; this time he legitimately is at work rather than locked up. But ironically the work he is doing is in construction, putting the roof on the new prison. He and I have discussed over the phone the idea of me moving up there to have a better run at my senior years of school, and the plan was I would go at Easter. My grades are good enough that Dad is confident I might get a scholarship for the private school near his apartment.

Approaching home, I spot Mum in the front yard. She is throwing things in the car, and Taylah and Max are already home. I am confused. They aren't in their school uniforms, and Mum is frantically chucking blankets and bulging striped bags into the car. Why is she rushing? Spotting me she begins to yell at the kids to get in the car.

I pick up my pace and walk up to her, examining what she has packed.

'Mum, what's going on?'

'I'm going to spend some time with your father before you get up there and turn him against me for good,' she hisses at me.

Ah, she is in one of those moods. Sometimes Mum becomes convinced that I am her enemy, that rather than my time being spent at school and working shifts at McDonalds, I am in fact dedicated to plotting for her demise.

She jumps in the car. Max and Taylah are already in their seats; they wave at me and blow kisses as she reverses. Stepping aside I wave back to my younger siblings. It's no good arguing with Mum right now, and a few weeks without her here will mean I can actually stay at school until the bell rings. The teachers are starting to get suspicious, and I reckon some of them think I'm sneaking out to smoke.

I walk into the main house, throwing down my bag and heading to the cupboard. Damn, she *was* in a manic high mood today; the cupboard is full of food, a sight I have almost never seen. She has intentionally bought a couple of weeks' worth of shopping.

I smile to myself, and grabbing a packet of chips and a can of soft drink, pick up my bag and head out to the garage where I sleep. I lay on my bed, homework books spread out in front of me, enjoying the unexpected peace and snacks.

Two weeks pass, and no-one calls me in that time. I figure I best check in with my family; I am worrying about Taylah and Max. I don't even know if they arrived at Dad's. The home phone has been restricted to incoming calls only for years but I bought myself a mobile phone when I first got my job at McDonalds and today I have credit.

I call Dad first – the number I have dialled is disconnected. Hmmm.

I try Mum next – that number, too, is apparently disconnected.

I try Lisa, last I heard she was living in Sydney. Her number doesn't ring either but that's not unusual for her. She's twenty now and often drops off the radar and appears after a few months. I can't get hold of Mum or Dad. Nobody calls me.

Weeks and then months pass. Each day I walk home from school and listen out for sounds in the house as I walk down the driveway. But every day is the same: silence. Thankfully I have regular shifts at McDonalds, and can walk myself there and back, meaning that I have some money coming in for food because the snacks and drinks Mum had bought have all gone.

Easter comes, and goes, and I see no-one: not Mum, not Dad, not Lisa, and certainly not the Easter Bunny. I spend a lonely day at home, and when school resumes I lie and tell my friends that my family and I went on an Easter picnic. My phone doesn't ring and, strangely, bills that had been piling up stop coming. After a while, with fewer and fewer bills arriving in the mailbox, it occurs to me that Mum or Dad has had the mail redirected.

At fifteen I am one of the youngest in my grade, and I am pretty sure I am the only one living alone. Some weeks I don't get many shifts at work, and I struggle to eat a meal every day. I run out of basics like washing powder, and when winter comes, I get uniform penalty slips every day at school because I can't afford to buy any clothes, and the only jumpers I have don't meet the uniform code.

In class the teachers are driving home the pressure that we have to do well in the Year Ten Certificate; this will impact our options for our senior years, and our senior years impact whether we get into university. My mental health begins to spiral.

One day, when I am sitting out of PE because I do not have the correct uniform, the PE teacher, who is also our year-level adviser, Mrs Sparks, quietly comes up to me while the rest of the class are attempting the beep test.

'Amy, you know, if there's something going on, something you need help with, maybe trouble at home, you could tell me.'

I stare at my feet and don't say anything.

'If you trust me enough to tell me, Amy, I promise I won't tell anyone and maybe I can help you.'

In that moment, I break: the soothing tone of her voice, the offer of help from an actual adult is too tempting. I start to cry. I tell her about the fact that my family has moved away and not taken me with them. That it's been months, I have no address for them, no phone number, and I am desperately worried about my younger siblings. I can't afford a uniform, and keep getting penalised for it as though it's a choice, and I am hungry. It pours out of me in a stream like the tears that run down my face.

I take a deep breath and looking up into her face, I immediately see I have made a mistake. She looks horrified. She looks exactly how someone looks when they are about to go and repeat everything you just said.

Mrs Sparks takes a deep breath and says, 'I am so sorry, Amy ... I didn't expect ... I thought ... I have to report this.

I am a mandatory reporter, you're fifteen, I have to tell the principal.'

Immediate regret. I hate this place. I fucking knew I couldn't trust any of the teachers here.

She leaves the hall. She is back in a minute with another teacher, who takes over observing the rest of the class, who haven't noticed our conversation and continue trying to outrun the machine and its scheduled beeping. She instructs me to follow her, and I am tempted to tell her to go fuck herself, or to simply walk away. But I am too tired, and I can't quit school – I want to go to university. Shoulders dropped, heart full of regret, I pick up my bag and follow her to the principal's office.

She goes in ahead of me, leaving me in the hallway. The office-admin ladies peer over at me, already anticipating the gossip they will be able to share in regards to the impending meeting.

The principal's door opens and I am invited in. I sit on a chair beside Mrs Sparks. The door closes once more behind us, and the principal gazes over at me like I am an injured puppy.

'I am sure you understand, Amy, that what you have shared with Mrs Sparks puts us in a difficult situation. We have no choice but to report this to community services. You are still a child.'

Whatever I was expecting, it wasn't this. I try to object. I explain that *really I am fine*, and maybe if she could just instruct my teachers to stop giving me penalties for not having my uniform, we can pretend this never happened.

She is nodding but not listening to me. Putting the phone on loudspeaker, she dials, explaining as she does, that she wants me to be able to trust her and Mrs Sparks. To understand they are on my side, that we are a team, so she wants me to be present for this phone call. I have never wished harder for the earth to swallow me up. If I could have willed myself into non-existence in that moment, I would have.

Fifteen minutes of discussion later and I sit and watch, slightly amused, as the principal argues with the social worker who, after asking if I appeared to be in immediate danger (no), whether I was attending school regularly (yes), then went on to sum up the entire community services' response in a single line. I doubt she would have uttered it if she had known the entire discussion was taking place on loudspeaker and in front of me: 'I don't know what to tell you, we won't be getting involved, nobody wants a teenager.'

With that, the phone call ends, and the three of us sit in silence. The principal seems embarrassed, if anything, and I am dismissed from the room without any offers of practical support – no free uniform, no money for food. The only thing they achieved that day was to confirm for me that I could trust no-one.

For the rest of the day students with notes are sent to my classrooms telling me to accompany them to various staffrooms. It becomes abundantly clear that not only did Mrs Sparks breach my trust by reporting my story to the principal; she's gone ahead and told the entire staff body.

I get pulled out of class no less than a dozen times over the next few days. Each time I am met with nothing more than patronising facials and the words: *I am here if there's anything I can do.* What good is that to me?

Not one of the teachers considered that at fifteen years old, I have no way of articulating what I need. That with my most basic needs beyond shelter not being met, I would feel completely too shame to ask them for food or money, and none of them offer those anyway.

After two days of being sent for and word getting around, the other students in Emerald know something is going on. At lunchtime I am hounded by kids from across my year who want to know what I have done. I have nothing left in my emotional tank and end up screaming at everyone, threatening a few with violence if they didn't shut up and get out of my way. I storm out of the school grounds and walk home. By the time I am back in my garage, I determine I am going to have to change schools once I finish the Year Ten Certificate.

The school year ends with no introduced support by the school, and no appearance or contact from my parents. In the lead-up to the Year Ten Formal I work every shift I can get in order to pay for my ticket so I might attend. I search high and low until I manage to find a pair of shoes and a dress for under $50. On the day of the formal, one of my managers comes over to my garage when she finishes work and styles my hair. Another friend loans me her make-up, and a guy who I had made friends with at the local Video Ezy drives me and my date, a friend also in Emerald, to the event.

I end up doing well in the Year Ten Certificate – knowing but not telling anyone I won't be coming back to that high school.

In the holidays, my friends, guessing that I had in fact lied about the Easter picnic, convince their parents to do a 'Friends Christmas' and we all meet in a local park. They have chipped in and bought me some new swimmers and clothes as a present, knowing I couldn't get them anything in return. My whole life I have been blessed with rich and loving friendships.

That night I stay over at a friend's house, and when I arrive home on Boxing Day, I find my parents and siblings are back. I am so shocked to see my whole family when I walk in. But not as shocked as I am to discover that I am in a world of trouble for not being home for Christmas. Instead of apologies or explanations, I am met with screaming and abuse: how dare I not spend Christmas Day with my family? The fact I hadn't seen or heard from them for almost a year apparently not a relevant factor in my decision-making.

A few weeks later it is my sixteenth birthday, and though they're all back home now, I get no presents and no cake. I go to bed angry that I had been foolish enough to hope for better.

18

ADDICTION, SOBRIETY AND THE SPACE in between move like seasons. As a child, when your parents both struggle with addiction to a substance as intensely all-encompassing as heroin, there's no single signifier of where they are in their journeys. Instead, the entire home, the whole environment, shifts and changes depending on the phase in which they exist. You have as little control over their journey and your life as you do the weather itself, and spend your days hoping for calm and gentle sunshine, while doing your best to survive the big storms.

When they are deep in the grasp of using there is no money, little to no food, the house soon becomes a pit of filth, and you hope and pray each night that any or all of your grandparents will appear to either whisk you and your siblings away for a few days, or visit for long enough that some order is restored.

Sometimes the hopes and prayers are answered, sometimes they aren't; but within those seasons there is a certain peace and quiet that accompanies your parents being on the nod. They might rise to also pull cones, and there will be no spoons in the kitchen. But mostly they just lay around, eyes closed, head nodding down to their chest, and you and your siblings do your best to care for one another and get on with the business of being children.

When syringes are left in the bathroom, you carefully move them up high so the younger siblings won't play with them. When bongs are left on the floor, you move them to a shelf or atop the fridge knowing that there is no worse stench than spilt bong water.

When both your parents are hanging for a hit but unable to fund it – or attempting to make it through withdrawals as they seek out sobriety – they are unpredictable, and on occasion violent. Those are the only times when home doesn't generally feel safe. Voices and tempers rise, objects get smashed, and it will be like this for several days.

If they make it through those days, ideally landing in a season of sobriety rather than backsliding, there will soon be food in the cupboard and milk in the fridge once more. But they do not often make it through, and in these kinds of stormy times, you walk on eggshells and do your best to go unnoticed.

It is hard to be unnoticed as a child in a small home. One day, when Dad is away somewhere and Mum is in a rage of withdrawals, my older sister and I, aged fourteen and nine, retreat to the front bedroom to avoid Mum. We come to fight over something inconsequential; maybe it is over who had control of the radio station on the device we were playing at low volume. In any case, our whispered argument becomes a silent match of wrestling and pushing, when a timely shove from Lisa causes my head to connect with the bunkbed post. It is a decent hit and I let out an involuntary screech.

That screech will *not* go unnoticed. We've fucked up, we immediately freeze, eyes locked on each other as we listen to the sound of Mum stomping towards the room. She enters in a rage and we spring to stand apart from one another.

'What happened?' Mum looks ready to destroy something.

'She pushed me and I bumped my head,' I say, pointing my finger at Lisa.

'She's lying,' says my sister.

Mum's eyes narrow and she stares at each of us in turn.

'One of you is lying. Which one is it?'

'Not me!' we yell simultaneously, watching as Mum withdraws her leather belt from the loops on her jeans. This one has a shiny buckle on it.

Mum focuses on Lisa. Just as I begin to think it won't be me this time who cops it, she says to her, 'If Amy is lying, she will be punished.'

Lisa looks at her and with a straight face says, 'I am not lying.'

'Okay.'

Mum has the belt above her head and brought down onto me before I can hit the deck. But I do so as quickly as I can, rolling into a ball and pressing myself into the floor. The smaller I am, the less of me she will be able to reach. She begins to count each blow as she hits me. 'One, two, three … thirteen, fourteen, fifteen …'

Lisa can't stand it anymore and screams, 'It was me! I'm the one who is lying.'

Mum stops. I have mentally left my body but return to it now and lift my eyes to see Mum has paused, belt raised above her head. She lowers it slowly, out of breath from the force and action of belting me. She threads her belt back through the loops on her jeans. Then looking at Lisa she spits out, 'You make me sick' and walks back out of the room.

I remain in a ball on the floor. Lisa sits down beside me, crying and wrapping an arm over me tenderly, and whispering, 'I'm sorry'. But it is not her I hate in that moment. We both know I have said similar lies to avoid Mum's temper myself. I don't blame her. I just cry as quietly as I can.

That was a particularly bad season, and it would be incredibly easy to paint Mum as the villain when I consider my mid-to-teen years, but her mental health had reached extremes when we are living in Lake Macquarie. We are so far away from her family and support network, and though at one point she is formally diagnosed, she regularly neglects her prescribed medications. 'I don't want to be a zombie' is all she will say when we push her to go back to her GP and back on her meds.

In that season, to me she often felt like she was other-worldly, not quite present. She was *physically* present though, whereas Dad would often physically leave us. Back then, I always assumed when he was gone it was because he was away for work. As an adult I would come to discover that while *sometimes* he was in fact off at work, other times he just didn't want to be around Mum's mood swings, and so he would go and move in with his dad, leaving us behind.

Another time, Mum is doing well and has a job as a bartender a few suburbs over. She loves tending bar and is a favourite with the regulars. Her uniform is all black; but Mum prefers colour, so she joyfully shows me that she has taken to wearing bright coloured socks, and even if it's not visible she would know colour was there.

Dad is living at home with us again. He goes to work during the day, returning in time for her to go to work in the evenings. A rhythm develops and there is some flow but soon it becomes clear that Dad is struggling. His mood becomes dark and stormy, and one night when Mum is at work and my younger siblings are asleep, he is acting strangely and doesn't want the lights on.

I retreat to my bedroom that I share with my older sister; I know better than to try to watch television or risk being visible when he gets like this. Our grandparents, my dad's mum and his stepfather, had recently made beautiful wooden four-poster beds, complete with sheer curtains and colour-coordinated bedding for Lisa and me. Our room now looks like princess quarters in a castle. I approach my beautiful four-poster bed only to discover that my bedding is on my sister's bed, and her blankets are missing.

'Lisa! Give me back my blankets,' I hiss-whisper.

'No. Go find mine and use them if you want a blanket.'

This is bullshit. So I attempt to pull my blankets off her bed, but she is far stronger than me and I fall to the ground. We begin to argue, as I continue to pull on the bedding from the ground and she heaves back from up on the bed.

It has become a game of tug of war; we are each so wrapped up that we do not hear Dad storming into our room. He switches the light on and is yelling. Standing at six-foot-five, he is a scary figure as he demands to know what the hell is going on and why are we fighting.

We both attempt to shout over one another, but I am stopped short by Dad who has reached down and yanked me by my hair from the ground to a standing position.

'Where is her blanket, Amy?' he demands.

He seems to think I have taken her blanket, and he is not interested in anything other than an explanation of where it is.

'I don't know!'

He hits me with such force that I land back on the ground. Lisa is silent. We are both shocked. This is a new extreme for him, even in a bad season.

'Get her blanket now!'

I stand back up and again attempt to say I have no idea where it is, when his hand smacks me right in the face. I stop trying to argue and scramble away to start searching. I drop low and check under the beds – nope, not there. I decide to stay low and crawl as fast as I can into the next room. Most of the house lights are off and I legitimately have no idea where her blanket might be so I am panicking as I shuffle along the ground looking for signs of the bedding.

Dad follows me, raging.

I make it through two more rooms and finally come upon the blanket by the back window. Lisa must have been laying on it there earlier that day.

I grab the blanket and, getting to my feet, attempt to run past Dad, but he reaches out and his hand connects with my back, knocking me down once more. He has the energy of someone vindicated, as though me finding the blanket proves I had taken it initially.

'Now swap the blankets and tell her you're sorry,' he says.

'I'm sorry,' I lie, pulling my blanket off her bed and swapping it for her own.

Dad turns the light off and leaves the room once more. I climb into that princess bed and think to myself that princesses never get treated like this; I don't deserve this bed, I am no princess. I begin to resent the bed, its curtains, and the bedding that was bought to match it.

The next day Dad is clearly using again and back on the nod. All is calm and quiet in the house. Dad never apologises for that night but he also never hits me like that again.

Later that week I hear my parents talking about *something needing to change.* Mum is thinking about going to TAFE to study; they're worried about Lisa, about her schooling, and Dad is having a hard time with work.

A few months later they send Lisa to live interstate; she moves in with our aunty and uncle – new space, new opportunities. We remain behind on Awabakal Country – now it will just be me, Tay and Max with our parents.

19

I, FOR ONE, DIDN'T SEE that day coming – the one that changed everything in my life for a time. In the midst of the many storms that had raged around me – and there had been so many – home had mostly been a place of refuge. While my life was marked by inconsistency as the norm, I could always rely on the consistency of shelter. Until one day, I couldn't.

If I thought life was hard at home that was nothing compared to life without one. Homeless. It will be years before my parents and I speak of that day – or even speak to each other. And no matter how many times that day is discussed, we will disagree on what was said and done, and whether or not I should have believed that I had to leave. Whether Dad told me to go or not, or whether Mum spat or not, neither Dad nor Mum came after me. I will be in my twenties before they ever invite me back home.

I rise before the sun and walk the kilometre to work. I didn't want to get out of my warm bed this morning; it is nestled in the garage where it is dark and basic. It's my own little place in the world, and I feel safe there.

Today is 26 January, a public holiday, which means penalty rates at work. I hate everything about this day but am desperately grateful for the boost today's shift will give my pay. I have grown taller over the summer, and with school back in a week, I need money for a new school uniform and shoes.

We have new staff hired for the summer holidays; the additional people in an already small workspace is irritating me. As hard as it was being alone at home last year, having my family back home is proving difficult and unpredictable. Work is usually a bit of an escape but the increased number of staff in my workplace means I also feel suffocated there.

This is partly why I don't mind doing the open and close shifts. When I am on open shift, there will just be a few of us, until the morning rush begins when more staff arrive; so it's a slower, quieter start to the day.

We don't have work showers or even a staff bathroom. There is just a small room with open pigeonholes where we have to leave our personal belongings; it operates on a trust system. And so I place my small handbag, complete with wallet and phone, on a shelf and clock in.

Today I am on drive-through, and as the weather heats up so do the tempers of the customers. All day I serve people in cars draped with Australian flags, many of them intoxicated and wanting ice cream and milkshakes. The ice cream-slash-milkshake machine regularly breaks on hot and busy days; today is no exception. The ice machine is also struggling to meet the demand of today's rush.

I am inevitably yelled at by customers who want the unavailable shakes, the thirty-cent ice cream cones, or extra ice in their Cokes. The voice in my headset is constantly reminding me I have to tell the customers they can't have what they want.

The rush means I work on my feet for hours without a break, and the overcrowding of staff means there is nowhere to sit when I finally do get to stop. I decide to sit in the tiny public restroom for my fifteen minutes.

When it is finally time to clock off for the day, I drag myself out of the drive-through booth, handing the headset to my replacement, and grab a cup of water before stepping into the room of pigeonholes. My bag sits open, on its side – my wallet and phone are clearly missing. Someone has stolen my things.

The manager says they have no power to search other staff members' bags. Several staff have come and gone in the time I have been working, so there's nothing they can do. No compensation, no replacement. Nothing. Fuck.

I leave and walk home in the late afternoon, completely deflated. The $20 I had put aside for food this week was in my wallet, and being a public holiday, I can't even go into the bank to access the little money I do have. I feel physically weighed down as I walk along the footpath that runs behind the shopping centre, eventually bringing me out onto our street, the one with my primary school at the opposite end.

Our car isn't in the driveway so I walk into the house, grateful for a moment of silence. I sink into the couch and take some deep breaths. I need my next few pay cheques for this year's school shoes and uniform. I am now going to be without a phone for months maybe; considering I often walk the kilometre to and from work in the dark, I don't like how vulnerable that leaves me.

The sound of a car pulling into the driveway rouses me from the half-sleep I was falling into. I instinctively go to get up and retreat to the garage where I sleep; but thinking about the loud complaints Dad has been making lately about me *not acting like part of the family*, I sit back down. I better stay and say hello, ask them how their day was.

Taylah and Max run in. They're sun-kissed and excitedly begin to show me the shells they have collected at the beach. Lisa walks in behind them; she doesn't live here anymore but is back here for some reason – holidays, I guess. Lisa has a grocery bag in hand, and I note that everything she is wearing belongs to me. Except for the skirt: *that* skirt is my friend Holly's.

I stare at her in shock – she has obviously gone through my things after I left for work.

'Lisa, what the fuck?'

She looks over at me as she places the grocery bag on the kitchen bench.

'What?' Her tone is questioning but she is grinning smugly. She knows exactly *what*.

I don't have the energy to fight, and these days our fights always turn physical, so I decide to choose my battles. The priority is Holly's white skirt, which is small on me so absolutely too small for Lisa to be wearing.

'That skirt isn't mine, Lisa. I don't want you to ruin it. Take it off!'

'Make me,' she retorts, hands on hips.

She is being more playful than aggressive but my temper flares.

'Take the fucking skirt off, Lisa — your fat arse is stretching it to all fuckery.'

Mum walks in, skin a deeper brown than normal, sarong tied at her waist; but she doesn't seem relaxed. I have no idea what her mood was before she entered the house but hearing me raise my voice at Lisa, she walks over to where I sit on the couch and she spits on me. This is extreme even for Mum. I am shocked into silence.

Lisa's eyes widen. She quietly walks over to the washing pile that is heaped next to the kitchen bench, extracting a pair of sweatpants and slipping Holly's skirt off.

With that, the fight should be over but Mum is just getting started. I retract physically back into the couch as she stands over me and begins to yell profanities and names at me. Stopping every few words to again spit on me.

I have no fuel left in my tank — I want out. I wish I had just escaped to the garage when I heard them pull up. I wish I could escape completely. I know if I try to stand up now she will likely hit me and even though I am now taller than her – and probably stronger – I don't want to be hit and I won't hit her back. I stay seated, willing my body to sink so deep into the couch that I might just dissolve into nothingness.

She spits on me again, and my rage rises.

I spit my own verbal venom back at her.

'You are an animal,' I say, looking her dead in the eyes from my spot on the couch.

Uh-oh, terrible timing. Dad has walked in, just in time to hear me calling Mum an animal.

He storms over and adds his verbal assaults to the mix. He is raging. Together they're yelling at me simultaneously and I can barely hear what they're each saying. The words jumble together like ingredients thrown into a mixing bowl when making a cake. They blend and fold and soon all of the ingredients are indistinguishable from one another.

Dad seems to be railing against the fact that I don't spend time with them *as a family*, and Mum is yelling something about my *disgusting attitude*. I am so deeply tired.

I try to argue about the skirt, about the fact that they left me for a year, that my wallet and phone were stolen, and that I *just can't* today. That I work so much and I am so tired, that it's hard to spend time with them when there are six of us and the car only fits five, and they only seem to plan outings when they know I am at work. But nothing I am saying hits them.

Until I mutter: 'I hate it here.'

They both register this line but it is Dad who is fuelled into the next level of rage by it. He is pointing his finger at me, spit flying from the sides of his mouth. 'Then leave! Get out! You're not welcome here and we don't want you.'

'What?'

'Get the fuck out, Amy. Leave!'

I am not 'Lou' today. I stand up from the couch, ducking as I walk past them, anticipating a blow but they don't raise a hand. I walk out the back door through the backyard and into the garage where my bed is.

Closing the door behind me I lay down on my bed. I have nowhere to go, no wallet, no phone; so I just stay on the bed and shut my eyes for the moment – hoping their anger and the direction to leave will simply fade away.

It could be that a few minutes pass or maybe it's an hour – without my phone and with my eyes closed I have no sense of time – before a loud banging on the door brings me back to reality.

It is Dad; he is hammering on the door and yelling.

'Hurry up, you think I'm joking? Pack your bag and get the fuck out.'

Shit, he is serious. I start to cry but I quietly get up from the bed and glance around the room. What do I need and what can I carry with me? I can't see I'll be allowed back anytime soon, so I have to take what I need in one go. I look at the bright coloured blanket I bought with my tax return this past year, and the matching curtains. I look at my collection of ceramic houses. I won't be able to carry any of it.

I throw some clothes and toiletries in the only bag I own, with Dad hammering the whole time and yelling to hurry up and get out.

I open the door and he is standing right there.

Moving towards him I meet his energy and scream, 'ALRIGHT! I AM GOING!' before walking around the side of the house towards the street. As I open the side gate I see that Taylah and Max are watching from the front window.

Max is panicking. He runs through the front door and grabs my hand. 'Amy, stay, you don't have to go. I will hide you in my cupboard and you can have half of my dinner every night.' He is crying.

I give him a kiss on the head, tell him I have to go. Then pulling away from him I head out onto the nature strip and start walking back towards the path that runs behind the shopping centre.

The whole time Dad just stands at the side gate watching me leave.

As I set off down the street I think to myself maybe, maybe, if I walk far enough down the path and wait, they will calm down and come after me. I don't want to leave; I have nowhere to go, and this is my home. I walk along the path I had taken home from work earlier and, stopping halfway, find a tree to sit under.

I sit by that tree with my bag and wait. The sun is going down, the kookaburras begin their calls as the treetops turn golden. No-one comes along the path. I sit alone as it gets dark, the sound of crickets keeping me company.

Okay, well, that didn't work, they're serious. I realise they're not coming to get me. I stand up, putting my bag over my shoulder, and decide to head back to McDonalds. I don't even have money to call a friend from a payphone, so I will need to ask my manager for a loan.

I do my best to wipe my face and be presentable before I enter my workplace. Approaching the manager, I ask if we can talk in the small office. The large glass window facing the kitchen means there is no privacy but I tell her I've been kicked out of home, and she offers me money. I only take $20 because I am worried about borrowing anything I can't pay back. The evening rush is kicking off at work; so I get out of there, walking down to the shopping centre. There I call a friend, and they say that if I get the bus to their house I can stay with them tonight.

PART
TWO

20

T HE HARDEST PART OF A childhood with parents who have these struggles and are criminalised isn't necessarily life inside your home – it's how you are treated and mistreated by those outside your home. It's the ways in which people with authority disrespect, demean and dehumanise your whole family.

In childhood I am of my family, they are of me. We are treated collectively, and collectively we are assessed to be worthless. At the shops, whether with them or shopping alone, I am followed by security. The grocery store staff hover but never help. I am watched keenly but never seen.

Therefore, in becoming homeless and being separated from my family, this wasn't liberation; it simply brought me that much closer to the edge. It meant couch surfing, sleeping rough, missing days of food rather than simply missing individual meals, and feeling completely lost and cut out of social loops.

I did my best to hide being homeless. I didn't miss shifts at work, I kept going to school, and I told no-one. But word got out, and the parents who heard feared that I was prime to be the 'bad influence' that popular culture teaches parents of adolescents to fear. The worst part of being homeless, though, was being away from Taylah and Max.

For the first few weeks after I become homeless I couch surf, staying with friends and acquaintances until their parents say I have to leave. One person lets me know I can stay if I pay rent but they're asking for more than I make each week at McDonalds, so I have to leave.

I don't want people to know I have been kicked out. It is already hard to be known as the kid whose parents are addicts, and to be poor. But if you are kicked out of home as a teenager everyone assumes there is something very wrong with you. People barely notice me as it is – this will break the limits. Being the homeless kid will render me invisible and unworthy.

The bank issues me a new card but I remain phoneless as I can't afford to replace it; so I spend as much time as I can at either school or work because I have nowhere else to go. I don't want people to know I am homeless, but I also have no home. It becomes increasingly hard to make sure my work uniform and school uniform are clean.

Eventually, a friend who isn't willing to ignore the state I am clearly in, takes me into a community services office. There we sit with a social worker who goes through a list of services that might be available to me as a recently turned sixteen-year-old girl who is still attending school.

The social worker seems kind and genuinely committed to getting me support. But after going through all of the options, determines that while there is a shelter I could get a spot in, it isn't on a regular transport line. The shelter is too far from both school and work to be of use to me, given I have neither car nor driver's licence. She acknowledges that not being able to get to school and work will likely derail the remaining sanity I have. The shelter is taken off the table.

We go through the Centrelink forms together, and she makes calls on my behalf as I sit in her stuffy office. At the end of the day, unless my parents confirm that I can't live with them, it seems I can't receive any Centrelink payments. The Centrelink staff member makes contact with my dad, but when he refuses to cooperate I am told I have no options unless a family member is willing to go on record as saying the family home isn't safe. That would put custody of Taylah and Max at risk; so no, I don't think any extended family member would agree to go on the record saying that.

I leave the community services office with a voucher that allows me to spend two weeks at a local budget motel, and nothing else. A bed to sleep in for now is at least something, I think to myself.

The social worker walks me to the motel and sorts things out at reception. After that, I am left to my own devices once more. Settling in to the room, I decide to handwash my underwear and the pits of my work and school shirts in the motel sink using the free bar of soap. I have neither money nor transport to access a laundromat. Hanging the poorly washed clothes over the bathroom rails, I sit on the bed and try to do my homework.

After couch surfing and sleeping in places I would rather forget, I hear through a friend of a friend that there is a room in Boolaroo that I can rent inclusive of bills for $90 a week. I make around $110 a week at McDonalds. So that will leave me with a $20 budget for transport and food, and the room is furnished by the woman who owns the home. It makes the difference between me staying in school for the remainder of year eleven.

It's hard but I settle into a routine there. The landlord is only home a few nights a week; she often cooks double when she is home, leaving a plate for me in the fridge.

At the end of that year living on my own, I'm on a phone call with Nan, my mum's mum. She tells me that if I agree to move to the Central Coast, Darkinjung Country, and rent a room from her sister, she will confirm to Centrelink that I can't live with my parents.

I don't want to move to the Central Coast – that means leaving my work and changing schools again – but I can't finish high school and keep working this many hours and skipping meals. Nan won't cooperate with Centrelink unless I do as she instructs, so I agree.

In year twelve I move in with Nan's sister, paying $50 per week and half of the utility bills. I am also able to access Centrelink study allowance. I leave my community, my work, my school, the places and spaces I know, to be able to eat and have a roof over my head.

It is hard, but worth it overall because at seventeen I successfully finish year twelve, and find out I have been successful in gaining a place at university.

21

'I DID IT!' I SCREAM AND jump as I run into Dad's place, almost tripping over his big dog, Sam, in my haste. Looking up from his dining room table, mug of coffee and newspaper in front of him, Dad is momentarily confused.

'The thesis! I'm done! I can submit!' I yell at him.

As the realisation of what I'm saying dawns on him, Dad leaps to his feet with such ferocity that the chair behind him is thrown backwards and lands with a clatter. I hear it but don't see it fall as I am wrapped up in a bear hug that knocks the wind right out of my chest and obscures my vision. As tall as I have grown, Dad is still taller.

My head is pressed into his shoulder as he says, 'I am so proud of you, Lou.'

Once he releases me from his grip, I take a breath and say, 'I drove straight over to tell you.' I give Sam a pat, his tail wagging and thumping against the table leg. 'Is Mum here?'

Dad points to living room and follows me in there.

Mum is laying on the couch, book in hand, looking at me with a smile and eyebrows raised. 'What's going on?' she asks.

'Our daughter is going to be a Doctor,' Dad declares proudly, turning to go put the kettle on.

I dance my way over to Mum, crying but smiling as I sing, *I did it, I did it,* to the tune of a cartoon theme song we have all heard a million times – thanks to the many children who now fill our lives.

Mum doesn't get up but she puts her book to the side and, sitting up, says, 'This is exciting. We need to think about what you can wear to graduation.'

'How long 'til you graduate, Lou?' Dad calls over the sound of the rumbling kettle.

'Oh, I dunno, a few months but I have to be examined and conferred first.' I have my phone in hand and turn it to show Mum the regalia I will have to wear.

'Red? Why are the robes red? I thought you wear black to graduation?'

'Yeah, it's a bit poxy but my uni is red for doctorates – red robes and a doctoral bonnet.'

We sit and gossip over coffee, Mum joining us at the table as we talk graduation outfits. Then Dad calls his dad to tell him I am finished.

Before I leave I slip the printout of the acknowledgements page of my doctoral thesis onto the table; texting them, so they know it's there to read after I have left.

I enrolled in the PhD program almost five years ago; but in truth, it's been a lifelong journey combined recently with working full-time and raising my children. Throughout it all my parents have supported me to the best of their abilities – through the highs and lows.

I turn eighteen the year I begin university, and I follow the only piece of advice I had ever been given about turning eighteen: I go and get a job in a bar. I haven't seen or spoken to Mum or Dad for two years now but Mum always said bar work is the best work, that the hours can be clustered at night and the pay is better than McDonalds. I juggle full-time study with working as much as I can at a local bar and nightclub, regularly finishing at 3:00 am.

After a while, for a cool $100, I manage to pick up a very basic, slightly rusted car – it's older than me – from a friend's stepdad. Nan sends me $200 in the mail to help cover the registration and I am finally on the road.

The car isn't much but it's mine, and the freedom of a car, along with a roof over my head, and finally being in the place that I had been focused on getting to for over a decade is indescribably beautiful to me.

My first day at university I see an academic procession for the first time. All of the commencing students are gathered and seated in the Great Hall when the music begins to swell, and a loud ceremonious knocking is heard throughout the hall.

Everyone stands. The doors open and in walk the academics; their thick, plush robes swirling around them, and on the heads of many are caps I have never seen before. These aren't like the usual graduation caps – the mortarboards – I've seen in the movies. These are rounded and come in different colours and look like something a character in a Robin Hood or King Arthur legend would wear. I am too shame to ask anyone what the caps mean or why they differ, so I quietly watch on in awe.

These must be the most important people I have ever seen in real life, and I am going to get to learn from them. It makes sense to me that this looks like a scene from *Harry Potter* because this feels like absolute magic.

Entry to university has been the goal for so long, so how to function when I get there is at first, a mystery. Once I learn to code switch between university language and home language, I realise that just like in school itself, I can be tested and measured here, and not be found wanting. As I grow and progress through my degree I am in and out of relationships, dating people here and there. But the one consistent for me is how much I love to study and learn.

I didn't know anyone who had ever been to university before I went, and most of the friends I make that first year still live at home with their own families. They aren't the first in their family to be here and they spend uni breaks travelling and going to music festivals. I spend my time away from campus working as much as possible, and organising to have Max and Taylah come to visit me for as many days as I can manage.

Those other students and I, we aren't the same. But I try to tell myself we all belong here, that I can be right for university and university can be right for me. In my classes I learn about literature from lands I didn't even know existed. We read together, analyse, and create our own worlds and works. I start to dream of being a writer, with writing-focused subjects far and away my favourites. In writing, I am moved in my mind beyond my circumstances, and released to dream beyond my everyday exhaustion. I yearn for new realities and opportunities.

I decide to go to church; I want to know more about the places my parents have never taken us and I have never been to church. As a result, I start having dinner on Mondays with a new group of friends; they are creatives, artists, small business owners, teachers, home owners and all belong to the same church that I begin attending.

My dad had raised me to understand that *it is better to die standing than to live life on your knees.* Here, with these people, I am told such an attitude is mean and misunderstands my role in life. I need to soften, to submit and realise that *life on my knees,* in service and submission, is true freedom. *Disrespect is simply an opportunity to practise forgiveness.* This goes against everything I've learnt; all I know is woven through poverty, and these people are well resourced. I want to know and understand more about their lives and how they manage them – I want resources. I want to find a way to create more and obtain more for my family: resources, healing, release within this life.

One night over dinner, I'm asked by my church friends what I hope to *be* when I graduate. Previously when asked this question, I had always answered 'lawyer' – my goal has always been survival. But my recent experiences with writing subjects have made me feel that maybe I could do more than just survive; that thriving was a possibility. In this group I thought maybe there would be understanding and encouragement for a new pathway.

With butterflies in my tummy, I answer, 'I think maybe I would like to be a poet or a writer.'

I was used to people being impressed and encouraging when I had answered 'lawyer'. But tonight at this table, these friends respond by *laughing*. I don't laugh with them. They attempt to soften their laughter with explanations.

'Maybe you could do it as a *hobby*, but you would have to be *really good* to actually make money from writing.'

Oh, that's right … of course. They're confident, bold and comfortably off; they must be right. I can't be a writer, and really, I was silly to think such a thing. I am an imposter, and these are people who can see that. They begin suggesting better goals for me, more appropriate careers. Maybe I should be a schoolteacher or a social worker, something where I can *help* people.

I repress my disappointment and laugh along with them. Yeah, I was just being silly. Silly Amy. I am not special enough to write. Instead I need to seek to serve, to find a role where I might make some money and help people. I push the desire to write deep, deep down, willing it to simply go to sleep, and return to focusing on survival. Thriving isn't for people like me.

When the day comes that I complete university, crossing that stage as a graduate with a Bachelor of Arts degree, I finally have the courage to ask someone about the strange academic caps.

'Why are some of the academics wearing those fancy caps?' I whisper to one of my lecturers as we mingle with cheap wine in hand after the ceremony.

They don't laugh at me; they answer seriously and with kindness.

'They're the academics who have PhDs, Amy. That cap signifies title not subject area – it means you have to call them Doctor.'

'And how do you become a Doctor?'

'You keep going to university.'

I decided then and there that one day I will cross that stage wearing my own velvet cap and with the title Doctor.

My parents and I slowly reconnect over my years studying for that first degree. We are on good terms by the time I graduate with my Bachelor's degree. But between us, we don't have the money to afford their tickets to graduation. Between us, we still have little to no money. The cost of my regalia hire and the tickets to the ceremony catch us all by surprise, and so that day I walk across the stage without them there.

But I do, as guided that day at my first graduation, and I keep going to university.

We are all more prepared by the time I complete my Master's degree. My family stand in the audience and cheer, cooeeing and hollering because they have no idea that's not what you do in places like this; and I for one would throw hands at anyone who tried to shame them for cheering on their daughter. They always knew I belonged in places just like this.

That's why in the acknowledgements to my doctoral thesis I printed out for them, they found these words:

This thesis grew around, within and alongside my life, meaning it became part of my family, and thankfully my family accepted and encouraged its presence ... My first teachers were my parents, Kevin and Debbie, and my grandfather Malcolm, each of whom instilled in me a deep love of learning. As I grew and began my journey as an early career academic, each of them supported me with their ardent encouragement and their unwavering belief that I not only belonged here in the academy but that I would excel. Thank you Mum, Dad and Pop. I have learnt and grown so much from your role modelling, your keen questioning and your listening ears.

22

M Y VIEWS ON LOVE AND relationships are shaped and shaken repeatedly. This continues today but happened most dramatically throughout my adolescence and early adulthood when I didn't talk to my parents for four years.

In that time, I fled far from my family's way of being and knowing and doing, seeking to rebel and separate; confusing measurable markers, such as church membership and access to wealth, with actual traits of respect, integrity and honour. In running so far, I allowed disrespect to seep into my life; I threw away the lessons that would have served me.

I allowed bad, unworthy men to propose and push mediocrity and violence. I accepted it, believing features that had nothing to do with character and everything to do with privilege, meant that they were better than me. I believed that with these men I would be freed from the systems that had said my value was non-existent.

I was wrong, and it took me years to come full circle and learn again those things that my family had already taught me many years before; that disrespect should never be tolerated; that criminal records or wealth (or the lack thereof) are not markers of a person's worth or heart; and that in building our own community up, we also build ourselves.

'If you were my girlfriend, I'd treat you like a princess.'

The sound of Ryan talking seeps into my ears and brings me back to reality. It is a beautiful sunny day and we are seated on the deck of a waterfront bar, lunch ordered; my boyfriend, Justin, gone to the bar to order drinks. I'd been looking out across the water, my thoughts far away and focused on a psychology assignment I was anxious to work on.

'What?' I say, sure I must have misheard.

'If you were my girlfriend, I would treat you like a princess,' Ryan repeats.

I frown, unsure how to take this remark. Ryan is Justin's best friend, and this is the first time in over a year of knowing each other that he's ever said anything like this to me.

'Ryan, you won't even let Emma keep a toothbrush at your house. I don't think Prince Charming is how many of your girlfriends would describe you,' I retort with a slight laugh.

We both know Emma is not technically his girlfriend. But making a joke is my primary response when I don't understand what is going on, and I'm hoping this will shift the direction of the conversation.

Before Ryan can respond though, Justin returns from the bar and places two schooners of beer on the table.

I look at the drinks, then look at Justin. 'Where's my drink?' I ask.

'Oh shit, I forgot!' he says, before settling into his seat and taking a mouthful of the beer.

I stare at him.

'What? You've got two legs – go get your own.' Justin laughs at himself as though he has just said something terribly clever. Ryan laughs too, but looks at me with an eyebrow raised.

I decide I will go get my own drink, to avoid an argument with Justin, and to get away from Ryan.

Ever since the weather warmed up, Justin and I have fallen into the habit of getting together with his mates on Sundays to have a few drinks. I don't mind most of the small crew but we see Ryan the most and something about him rubs me the wrong way. He often makes condescending comments when I talk. And as an ex-cop, he regularly attempts to regale us with stories of the ways in which he has manipulated the policing system, most of which seem to involve him intimidating junior officers into letting him off whenever he gets pulled over for drink driving or speeding.

I'd first met Justin through a friend at school. He was several years older than me, and there was no better way to describe him than as *comfortably mediocre*. He didn't seem to hold high ambitions, was still living at home with his parents, working retail in a local shopping centre, and completely uninterested in trying out university or learning a trade. He didn't even seem to want to dream ambitiously about fun things, shutting me down firmly whenever I tried to talk about my dreams of one day travelling to France. But he was mostly predictable and consistent, and so it hadn't taken long for me to fall into a relationship with him.

We finish our meals, and agreeing to one more round, Ryan goes to the bar this time. When he returns to the table, he places my drink of choice in front of me.

'Here you go, princess,' he says, with a wink.

If Justin notices, he doesn't say anything.

The following week Justin and I throw a house party. It's the first time we are intentionally bringing both of our social circles together. We've filled the fridge with mixers, beer and vodka, made a playlist, and set up Justin's laptop to pump through a speaker, which is definitely too large for this tiny townhouse. The neighbours won't like it, but I don't particularly like them so am not overly bothered.

Dusk settles, and with fairy lights twinkling over the front door, my friends from high school, university and work begin to show up. The only friend of Justin's to come is Ryan. We all drink and dance in the tiny living room late into the night, and in the comfort of my home, where the only people present are my friends, I drink more than I ordinarily would.

Sometime later in the evening, when conversations are in full flow, everyone is laughing, and Justin has ducked upstairs to the toilet, I walk between the lounge room and the kitchen in search of another drink. Suddenly Ryan steps into my personal space. Really up close in my space.

At first I think it is the harmless kind of moment when two people attempt to walk through the same gap, and instead walk into each other. But then I realise Ryan's hands are on my shoulders. He is pushing me back into the wall and trying to kiss me.

I duck the advance, turning my head away and saying 'no' but I'm unable to move away from the wall – he has me pinned. I am confused, and looking back at him I try to shout over the loud music, 'What are you doing?'

But as soon as I do, he once again attempts to press his mouth into mine. I turn my head away again, and he plants his mouth onto my jaw. His kisses are wet and forceful, his mouth travels along my jaw, and with his hot breath in my ear, he says, 'We both want this, you know we both want this.'

He has one hand firmly pressing my shoulder into the wall, while his other drops and begins to fumble at the top of my pants. He isn't trying to undo the buttons – he is forcing his hand between my belly and the material.

I am no longer confused. I am panicking now. Repeating 'no, no, no' as loudly as I can and attempting to wriggle out of his grasp. But I am too drunk, and he is too strong. His mouth is all over my jaw, my neck, up in my hair. His hot breath is still in my ear, as his hand slides down my pants, rubbing across my skin, over my pubic bone, feeling and forcing his fingers down and in.

It is then – right at the point of penetration – that the music suddenly stops. In the silence, the sound of my 'no, no, no' rings out clearly, and is the only noise I hear as Ryan is forcibly lifted off me.

Free from his grip, I slip down the wall and from the floor see that a couple of my friends' boyfriends have realised what was happening, and have killed the music and grabbed him off me. Someone turns the light on and I watch as the guys continue wrestling Ryan towards the front door.

'Alright!' he yells, and shaking them off, straightens his clothes and walks out the door willingly.

My friend, Lexi, comes over and sits beside me. 'Are you okay?' they ask.

I start to cry and am struggling to breathe.

After checking Ryan has definitely left, someone suggests we all go sit in the cool night air. It helps me feel like I can return to my body.

I sit in the moonlight, fairy lights still twinkling, and begin to breathe freely once more. I am there on the cold footpath when I hear Justin coming down the stairs.

He bounds out the front door all smiles and asks, 'What happened to the music?'

One of the guys who wrestled Ryan off me, steps forward and quietly explains to Justin that Ryan has assaulted me and they've had to kick him out.

I begin to cry again, somehow knowing in my belly what is coming next.

Justin looks around at us and declares, 'Bullshit.' He storms back inside.

The party mood has now significantly diminished. Those who aren't staying over head off and the rest of us return inside. I sleep on the couch that night, and Justin doesn't try to talk to me.

The next morning with the sun risen but everyone still asleep, we are roused by a knock on the door. Lexi, who has been sleeping beside me on the couch, puts a hand on my arm and whispers, 'I'll get the door.'

Before either of us can move, Justin comes down the stairs. He is already dressed and doesn't look at the small crowd sleeping in the living room. He opens the front door and there is Ryan.

Lexi sits upright. We are all awake now and quietly watching. Ryan says nothing.

Justin looks over at me and says, 'I am going to stay with Ryan for a few days. Let me know when you wake up to yourself.'

I can only assume this means he doesn't believe me, even though a house full of people saw the assault and physically intervened to make it stop. The front door closes.

Lexi leaves their hand on me, whispering, 'Amy, I want to

take you down to the station. I think you should report what happened to the police.'

I stare at my white friend. 'Babe, he basically *is* the police. The only thing I'm doing today is getting coffee.'

Justin and I don't talk for two days. Then he calls me and asks if he can stop in on his way to work. I agree, curious as to what explanation he will offer. I am in no way prepared for what he has come to say.

He arrives, dressed for work, and comes in carrying a bouquet of slightly wilted service station flowers. He doesn't seem fussed that there are people at home with me. Walking past them, he stops in front of me, and takes a knee.

My mouth drops open as he begins what is clearly a rehearsed speech, promising a trip to France, and a lifetime of loving me. A proposal. I don't know how to respond. There are people here, I am not expecting this; I need to think about it, and also I don't want to embarrass him. Embarrassed people are dangerous people.

'Can you come back tonight, after work? I need to think about it.'

He gets up from his knee, places the flowers on the kitchen bench and heads out the front door.

My friends who just bore witness to this unexpected display, stare at me with open mouths.

How the fuck do I navigate this? I get ready to go out to university for the day. While walking between the train station and lecture theatre, I decide that a handwritten note is the best way to decline the offer of marriage from a man who chose to stand by the man who just sexually assaulted me.

When I get home that afternoon I sit at the dining table and work on an assessment, nestling the handwritten note I have crafted in between my laptop and several textbooks.

When Justin arrives, I am mid essay. I get up and hand him the note before returning to the table. I don't say anything, and neither does he as he reads. I am sitting, facing my laptop, staring at the wall in front of me, when I hear him open the fridge door. I listen to the hiss of a soft drink bottle being opened. I don't turn around, assuming he is pouring himself a drink before responding to the note. But instead of hearing the cupboard door opening or a glass being set down, I feel cold liquid hit the crown of my head.

My body freezes as the fluid hits my eyes, and I close them to the sting of the sweet liquid. I don't move as soft drink runs down through my hair, hitting my shoulders, soaking my clothing, splashing the dining table and pooling on the floor.

When the liquid has finished pouring down and I can take a breath, I wipe my eyes and take in the scene. Justin stands, smiling, holding a now empty two-litre bottle of Solo above my head. My mind is unable to process exactly what is happening.

Before I can formulate any words or move my body, Justin

sprints not to the front door, but up the stairs and into the bathroom. I hear the linen closet open and then the shower is turned on. The shower is still running as he comes back downstairs. He looks at me and smugly says, 'Have fun washing that off', before walking out the front door.

Once I hear his car pull away, I get up and, stepping over the puddle pooled at my feet, go upstairs to try to work out what he has done. The linen closet door is still open, and I can see he has emptied it of all the towels. I walk into the bathroom and see they're all now in the bath soaked with water. I turn the shower off and stand in the bathroom; cold and as dripping wet as the towels.

I disassociate and am brought back to my body by my phone ringing. I walk downstairs to the kitchen and answer it. It's a friend, and I explain to her what Justin has just done. She drives over with a towel.

She helps me put my towels in the washing machine to spin the excess water out, wipes down the table, and mops the floor. Then, while I go for a shower, she searches: *how to clean library textbooks of soft drink*. I can't afford to replace these textbooks.

The following day my psychology tutor comes over to my house and I show her the damaged textbooks and tell her what happened.

She looks me straight in the eye and says, 'Amy, next time it will be lighter fluid. Promise me you won't see him again.'

I rub the top of my head and promise I'm done.

23

PUSHING DOWN INTO THE WATER, I release the air from my lungs in a slow stream, allowing my body to sink to the bottom of the ocean baths. I rest within the murky saltwater until my lungs can stand the deprivation no longer; then planting my feet I push up, breaking through the surface, gasping for air.

Taylah floats peacefully in the water beside me, unbothered by my sudden eruption. She waits for me to catch my breath and then casually remarks, 'Look up.'

There amongst the thin clouds floating past, highlighted against the dark pinks and blues of the evening sky, are shooting stars.

I sometimes wonder if Country sings louder when I'm with Taylah or if her sharply observational nature simply brings the singing to my attention; either way, these moments of magic aren't uncommon when we are together.

I have grown a community of loving friendships with good people who know how to hold space, respect boundaries, and show healthy love. And Taylah, as well as being my now-adult baby sister, is generally also one of my friends. Together we talk of cosmic interventions, timelines, divorces and crushes. We journey together through university, research, and the healing of wounds. Stardust above, stardust below, stardust within.

The further I travel into adulthood, the more I find there are few people outside of my family I can trust, and these days it takes a lot for me to trust. It wasn't always this way but lessons learnt over and over have left me wary of people in general, men in particular, something that Taylah understands.

The water of the ocean baths is still. So I lay backwards and relax my form until I'm floating alongside Tay – both of us now watching the lights overhead.

No doubt influenced by my Disney Princess obsession, I grow up believing that love is a castle. A towering creation, pre-built, immovable; an existing way of being that one day you simply receive and enter passively, possibly after being chased like Cinderella as she fled the ball. Such a love is a space you *inhabit* but don't necessarily actively contribute to or choose. When love finds you, you're simply uplifted. Absorbed into those towering walls, spending your days thereafter learning and navigating those corridors, being transformed into *their* world of tradition and practice.

What of Cinderella remained after she married the prince? Who was she outside of being that young woman he met, who was once trapped in poverty and servitude? We never know: her identity isn't storied beyond her relation to others, but we are told that she lives *happily ever after.* So my understanding was that, though a princess would enter that space with ease, they would also have to exchange their own conduct and rhythm, spending their time dressing, talking, and acting according to the rituals of their new love's home, their castle.

When the day comes that I first fall in love, I am an exhausted university student studying full-time, working late nights in a bar, and struggling to make ends meet. Doug's attention hits me in a whirlwind of song dedications and deluxe meals made with no budget in mind. I am drawn in and led by my senses, which fire off every time our paths cross. A combination of basic lust and a sense of *ease.*

It takes almost no time at all for love and violence to creep in amongst the meals. Increasing phone calls and text messages spliced with unkind words, and our time together accompanied by explicit instructions on what I should wear and how I should talk.

I become mixed up, finding my physical senses often in

conflict with my mind; one half says, 'Stay' while the other screams, 'Run, fast!'

But despite what I *see*, what I *hear*, this person *feels* safe to me. I just take a deep breath and no matter what has transpired, or how upset I am, in my belly I feel comforted when I am with Doug. Despite the physical and emotional pain that quickly accompanies almost all of our interactions, his love is a castle, and I am Cinderella, being uplifted – though the work of navigating new ways and behaviours will cost me.

It is only once we began to share a home that I suddenly realise the reason I *feel* safe is nothing more than a trick of my olfactory settings. Unpacking the moving boxes in the bathroom I discover that Doug wears the same cologne as my Pop Maccoll. He smells the way the safest man in my life smells. And for the price of a $9 supermarket bottle of men's aftershave, he's unintentionally triggered feelings of safety and deep love within me, even while he rains blows upon me.

People see a moat around a castle and talk about how it is there to keep intruders out. But once you're within a castle, it becomes clear the same moat will also act to keep you *in*. If love was a castle, as I breathed in that cologne I realised I didn't know how to escape it.

It would take me years to unpack the trauma of that first love, and even longer to recognise that truly love is not a castle.

I go on to complete university but I no longer wish to marry royalty. I grow to understand, if anything, love is more like a nest. A manifestation of natural, organic beauty, not imposed status; actively grown and nurtured, woven and made up of pieces collected and gifted from within an environment, a community. Each twig, leaf and piece gathered and connected with intention – coming together to form a safe, sound and perfect home for the season in which it is needed.

Love is moments such as floating in the ocean, watching shooting stars, and taking slow breaths. I am not trapped by – nor am I passive in – love's creation. I am a weaver, sometimes working alone, but always drawing upon the learnings role-modelled for me by my family and community.

PART
THREE

24

THE OCEAN AIR, SALTY AND cleansing, surrounds me. Waves of dragonflies cross my path as I walk with intention up and down the sloping pathway that leads from the ocean baths to the beaches. I find myself wondering if their fluttering wings are ancestors and Country reaching out to surround me, or if it is simply dragonfly season, and these pathways were built clumsily in their flight paths. Perhaps it is both of those things, simultaneously.

Today was too much before it even began; so I cancelled work, put on my runners and headphones, and came here. Here, where we played and walked and explored as children. Here, where the surf festival happens every year, an annual tradition our father marks by adding another festival-branded t-shirt to his collection and telling us all of his glory days riding waves.

It's also here, where the police officer rode past us as children, and turned around to accost us three sisters – aged fifteen, ten and four – because four-year-old Taylah had stuck her tongue out at him as our paths had crossed. Apparently the tongue of a small child was far too offensive to his sensitive ego to let go, and so he had aggressively turned around on his pushbike, and sprayed us with his rage and rebuking before turning again and riding away.

His words lingered like the salt and heat that day, and I think of his anger every time I walk across this particular intersection of beach and road. I had felt so intimidated by this grown man, weapon on hip, height well above my own.

I had watched my older sister, Lisa, be composed, quiet and submissive to his rage. I wanted to argue with him, tell him to ride on and get over it, but knew to instead follow her lead. She was calm, just nodded, and assured the officer she would chastise the preschooler.

He rode on, and she told Taylah, 'We don't stick our tongues out at officers.'

I watched and listened and would go on to unpack those lessons and dynamics for years to come. Even today, Lisa's the only one of us four kids who adamantly refuses to get an *ACAB* tattoo, though we younger girls have tried to convince her.

So it's ironic – I think that's the right word – that today as I walk and sweat and try to clear my head and heart in this salty air that it is my older sister who calls and asks that I proofread her statement detailing her account of an officer violently assaulting her earlier this year. She was left with her hand scarred, her shoulder damaged to the point of needing physio and painkillers, and with his threats to rip her hijab from her head still ringing in her ears.

When Lisa originally told us she was going to go down to the station, we told her: *You know what you need to remember when it comes to talking to the police – don't!* But it was supposed to be a routine meeting to discuss an item the police had wrongly confiscated; something that Lisa had proof of ownership for. After months of them running her around, it seemed a new officer was taking over the matter, and if she would just come into the station, it would be sorted.

But, she would tell us later over coffee, once they had her down there and in a room alone, nothing was sorted; it had become an interrogation, and they'd demanded her phone and passcode. When she refused to comply, the officer attacked her, another female officer piled on too, and the two of them left Lisa bloodied and wounded and terrified.

And now as I try to escape my own stress for the day, try to lessen the increasing anxiety that binds my chest, Lisa's voice is on the phone, in my headphones. I find myself taking a deeper breath and softening my voice as I assure her that of course, I can stop what I am doing to read her statement.

She didn't finish high school and is paranoid about her writing ability. Understandable. She emails it to my phone as we speak, and I sit on a low brick wall, the sun on my back, and read her words on the tiny screen. Her words are so powerful and my heart is absolutely aching at the violence of these systems that we must endure.

'I'm so sorry this happened to you – that must have been so scary,' I say to her as I read her statement over.

'Do you know what it was that was the most scary?' she says. 'That when I screamed for help, no-one came. Police are meant to help you. I've never been in trouble with the police, I tell the boys that if there's danger we call the police but … when I screamed for help no other officers came in and I know they could see and hear me.'

I am frustrated to learn she encourages my nephews to trust the police. This is so counter to every experience our family has had with them; so, while I shouldn't, I can't help but say it again.

'Well, you know what you need to remember when it comes to talking to the police – don't.'

She isn't impressed – it's not the time to push that point – and she really believed it would be fine. Her hand is scarred but the deeper pain is not the kind you can see from the outside. I wonder if she will get a payout. I hope so, but I doubt anything will come of it. Police investigate police, justice isn't something I associate at all with these systems.

We end the call and I continue with my walk, dipping between dragonflies and focusing on the rolling waves that crash along the coastline, as I try to breathe through my anxiety pains.

25

SOME FAMILIES MAY BOAST A legacy of generational wealth: assets including land, passed down alongside genetic traits, physical characteristics and social mobility inherited from their parents. For others, the legacy is that of trauma. What isn't talked about enough is that your inheritance isn't necessarily reflective of the amount of love, or the intentions that went into your raising. When we judge another's parenting, or when we view a family that is experiencing a lack of resources or an abundance of pain as a home that is lacking in love, we are often missing the context of a complex, intergenerational familial legacy that comes together in forming that home.

Though some parents and carers might say, 'You kids have it so easy' as a form of scolding, I hope to be able to make that claim on my own children because that is the whole point – that they have easier and healthier childhoods than I did. And when they're old enough I hope they will understand that generations of their people have worked at our own healing in order to provide them with that ease.

I'm driving home in the rain with my dad in the passenger seat. He's nervous about my driving; I'm nervous about the lecture I still haven't recorded that is due to be uploaded in six hours. It's the middle of the night, in the midst of a pandemic.

He and I headed out together earlier today after receiving the same emergency phone calls. A loved one in a bad situation: domestic violence. The neighbours called the ambulance, and the police had then taken the perpetrator away and were holding him in lock-up. We'd jumped in the car and hoped that her broken jaw and his temporary forced removal would mean she would finally be willing to get out of there. We tried to help her leave, but in the end she stayed and we left.

We tried – and maybe that's what matters. We will try again. But right now it's 3.00 am. We achieved nothing, and we still aren't home yet.

We're almost past some roadworks and you're talking about 'the ECL' – the East Coast Low. The lack of wind means the rain is here to stay for now. We start talking about Christmas, how last year it was a shitshow, and this year it will be at my house. I tell you about the new Lohmann Browns that I want to add to my backyard chicken flock.

That's when you start to tell me a childhood story.

'My mum stabbed this man she was seeing. He was howling. Her and the other three ran for the door, they made it through but he grabbed me. I was covered in his blood.'

I slow the car to eighty, then sixty, then forty, more roadworks. You've never told me this story before, and I wonder if Nan would tell it the same way. I read somewhere that driving is a good time to have these yarns; no eye contact, lots of quiet, minor distractions.

'How old were you?'

'Oh, I must have been eight. I was terrified. The police wouldn't come. God, he was howling and clinging to me.'

'Where did Nan stab him?'

'In the guts. It was Christmas Eve. The four of us kids got Mouse Trap as our one gift to share. We loved that game. It was all that we had.'

I don't ask what happened to the man.

Twenty-seven schools. Always being evicted, cared for by a single mother with no safety net. No single pension back then. Four kids, no food, moving from room, to shelter, to a water tank that one time. Men flogging her, men flogging kids. A good woman doing her best in extremely difficult situations. Your childhood was a kind of hell; one I have never heard Nan talk about.

That's when you tell me about the budgie.

Your voice drops. 'We were staying in one of those buildings – they sell for a lot now – what are they called?'

'Terraces? Like townhouses but flash?'

'Yeah, terraces. People were living downstairs. We were staying in a room upstairs. Mum's friend gave me a budgie, so young it didn't have all its feathers yet.'

I'm now thinking of the cockatiels and the chickens we had as kids; the fierce protection you show to animals, to your dog Sam, who sleeps on your bed.

Your hands are out in front of you, your eyes not seeing the car, as you tell me about how the budgie would hop on your finger. Your little mate.

'Mum was seeing this bastard and one night he comes in … they'd just gotten home from the pub.'

You're choking up. Fuck. Now I want to buy you a budgie.

'He came in, he took the cage outside and he got rid of the budgie saying birds don't belong in cages.'

'Did you ever see the budgie again?'

'No, he was gone. I was gutted.'

I don't know what to say, so I say nothing. We clear the roadworks and drive the rest of the way home in silence.

I drop you at your home just before the sun begins to rise. And as you always do, you say, 'I love you, Lou', before walking down your driveway.

I love you too, Dad.

26

THE JOURNEY OF RECONNECTING WITH my parents was a slow and clumsy one. It began with a desire to have them there for big moments – I missed them. It involved the realisation that while they had struggles, and sometimes those struggles had hurt me, unlike other people I met when away from them, they never sought to hurt me. Intention isn't everything, but their belief in me and their attempts to support me had been better than what I'd found in other homes and hearts.

Reconnecting with my parents, and *understanding* them, were two unrelated journeys. I didn't understand my parents, even when I started to reconnect with them. You don't have to understand fully to begin to accept in part, and I continued to be deeply resentful for many years, believing that they actively, consciously chose drugs over me. That it was a binary and I was the lesser option.

The resentment only began to ease in my late twenties when I was admitted to hospital and in so much pain that I was given a painkiller I would later learn is essentially synthetic heroin. I hadn't been exposed to opioids – synthetic or otherwise – since the womb. And it hit me with such force that the doctors initially thought I was having an adverse reaction, before eventually recognising that exposure in the womb had left me hypersensitive.

I was okay, just on the nod. It was a sensation I could never have imagined. I had always assumed that using must envelop you in some kind of feeling of bliss – that it must be akin to a really delicious meal when you are starving. That it would bring a sensation in and of itself. But I felt nothing. I entered a state of silence – everything within me that had previously always been so loud – went quiet.

That was when I began to understand that the nothingness is the bliss. My parents have experienced high levels of trauma – generational and individual – and all without the supports needed to actively heal. And when you carry high levels of pain – in your body, in your mind, in your heart – to suddenly be released into a state of quiet is like nothing else.

They weren't choosing heroin over me; they were choosing quiet over the overwhelming noise. It was then that I moved towards understanding, and my resentment began to ease a little.

27

I F ALL ENERGY IS ETERNAL, transformed, but never-ending, then I wonder as I sit on this sand and breathe this salted air if the spirits of my own children were also with us, all those years ago when we were children ourselves roaming tunnels and digging holes. Strawberry shakes with Pop, catching crabs, trying to catch flathead. When my soles were on this land, were their souls besides us, within us, ahead of us then, too?

I hold in my heart this space we were brought to in times of high anxiety, to give our parents a break, to shelter us from their storms. Awabakal Country: home of my birth, my lifeline, and today home to my children, my nephews, together. I sit, coffee in hand, as my eldest child learns to surf in a class that meets here, as it is the most sheltered of beaches on our coastline.

How slowly does rock deteriorate? Do the creation layers that caught my breath and felt my hands as I traversed and crawled and ducked within these cave walls back then feel these young ones now? Do they recognise we are of the same blood and energy and ancestors? Does the water know and remember us? That ocean swell, that washed over us in those days, and breaks now over these rocks, carving out these paths and nooks and lines that the children's feet walk over today, as they seek out life in the rock pools.

'AUNTY AMY!' their call rings out. Three bright faces beckoning me to look at the shells and rocks collected as we wait for surf lessons to end.

I'm cold as the winter air whips around us, but they are each too excited to feel it. Nguru created these mounds, and with their own leg created our ancestors, our great height from that creator spirit. We are neighbouring nations with a shared creator.

Surfing lessons come to a close, so one child is climbing out of a steamer suit and the other is out of my lap in order to chase his cousins, and together we move to check if the tide is low enough to enter the caves.

'AUNTY AMY!' they call out again, and their voices reverberate off the cold cave walls as we peer around and inside to see if it is safe, and whether we might enter.

That is when one falls, slipping into the water, a borrowed jumper he wears is filling and ballooning out, and as we laugh, I grab his little hand in mine to lift him out again, bright eyes sparkling and wide with the shock of it all. I see him as he was the day he became my son-nephew. My Zayd.

I had birthed Kael, your cousin, just weeks before you were born. Both of you, now brother-cousins, were barely months old when the call came to say your mother, my sister Lisa, was in danger – emergency surgery imminent. We rushed to be there at the hospital with you all.

When we arrived, Lisa was in an isolated room, and you were there beside her, screaming. You had never taken to a bottle. And though sedated and medicated, my sister was distressed because what they had already put in her system would be a risk to yours. So her breastfeeding you now was out of the question.

We rush in, collectively anxious, our overwhelmed thoughts pierced by your cries. You, me, my dad, your dad, and my then husband are all crowded around Lisa's bed in this room when the surgical team enter.

'He won't take a bottle,' Lisa says again, to no-one in particular, as your little form emits mighty screams and the surgical team indicate it is time to take my sister away.

My mind is filled with concern for Lisa – for what comes next – trying to listen to what the team are saying, when heat spreads across my chest: a letdown.

Your cries are triggering my milk. Your cousin is already fed and sleeping in the pram beside me, and the words are out of my mouth without a second thought: 'I can feed him. Breastfeed I mean, I have plenty of milk.'

All goes silent.

Then Lisa cries, relief. 'Yes,' she consents, all consent, and they wheel her out to surgery leaving us behind.

I pick up your crying little self and have you latched and filling your tummy before my dad, your dad, or my husband notice it has started.

The silence washes over us, and suddenly everyone realises I am breastfeeding you. While they are all in support, it feels unavoidably awkward; no-one wants to observe us, so they file out and leave me sitting in this strange hospital room with my son asleep in the pram, and you breathing deeply and suckling in my arms.

I trace your cheek with my finger and at some point, you realise that I am not her. You remain latched and keep drinking, but your bright eyes curiously search my face and then widen slightly. You *know* but continue anyway. I wonder if my milk tastes different to hers.

Five years on and my sister Lisa is safe. And you, my son-nephew Zayd, are strong; soaked through with the water of these beaches we swam in as children, standing in the opening of the very same caves that sheltered me and my siblings in the storms.

Together we share those memories and now build memories for your own futures. You are my son-nephew – energy transferred from my heart and myself to you.

28

ONE RECENT SUMMER, WHILE BUSHFIRES rage, the birds fall silent. For three days we don't hear or see them. Every morning and evening my children and I step outside into the heat and haze. We place containers of water wherever shade can be found, adding rocks and pebbles so that any critter who comes for a drink won't drown.

The closest fire is fifteen kilometres away and out of control. We are not in immediate threat from the fires here but the smoke is thick. I am worried about the wildlife, and our elderly neighbours. We've cleared the gutters and bought some drinking water, in case the town supply gets cut off. As we walk around the yard, what is left of the grass crunches underfoot.

'Mum, it's too spiky – there are bindis,' complains my son, as he hops behind me.

But there are no bindis – the grass is just dead.

Our home on Awabakal Country is nestled lovingly into Country, and out of every window we can usually see kookaburras, magpies, cockatoos, eastern rosellas, lorikeets, and tawny frogmouths. At night, possums run across the roof, making noises that make me think of pterodactyls. Our kin creatures visit us in the day, and in the evening come the bats, though I haven't quite figured out where they live.

This home is simple but it is my own. After years living away, I returned here to this Country deliberately – to raise my own babies on the lands where so much of my own learning has taken place. I walk my little block overlooking the lake; it's a safe space where I grow pumpkins, citrus and passionfruit in amongst the natives, and keep a small flock of chickens.

On weekends, for a treat, we might go and get McDonalds; the drive-through we go to is the very same booth where I once stood for hours taking orders as a homeless teen.

I now have an office in Sydney on the university campus where I am an academic. But I also work from home a couple of days a week, and on those days I drive to get coffee from a hole in the wall on the very street I once walked home alone in the dark, as a confused fourteen-year-old who didn't have a jumper or mobile phone to call for help.

I buy my family groceries from the same Woolworths I walked into with bong-water-soaked shoes, only $4 to my name, and desperate for supplies to see me through the dance festival. But now when I go through the checkout I don't even check the total before tapping my card. Some of the staff still there today were also there back then, watching me with eagle eyes when I was a kid, lest my desperation lead me to steal. Someone clearly never taught them the motto: *if you see someone shoplifting food, no you didn't.*

So much has changed but much remains the same. I intentionally live within the same community, celebrating holidays with my family, with my Elders, and returning what I have gained in the ways that I can. This is home but the way I experience these spaces has changed over time – I have caught up with my future echo. There is obligation, of course, but there is also an ease I never knew before.

This summer with the weather in the extremes, I think about the past as my children and I try to create safe conditions for the wildlife and our pets. We didn't have much when I was a kid, but we at least had rain and Christmas beetles.

Walking back inside and out of the smoky air, I pull down the blinds and begin to prepare morning tea. The smell of green apples – sharp and fresh – reminds me of childhood summers on Yuin Country. Pop cutting an apple into chunks, then holding me aloft, as I would hand-feed possums from the back step at Great-Grandma Lucy's house.

I smile, slicing the apple, and thinking of how we'd never try to feed the grumpy poss in the back shed – us kids were too scared to even go in there. I begin to story to my children about the way their Aunty Lisa and I would head down daily to swim in the waters now known as Shoalhaven River, tracking sand and dirt back up from the river and beach.

Their eyes sparkle as they question whether Aunty Lisa and I would just go off to the water alone. Without an adult? They have no idea how different their childhood is from my own, and I am not in a rush to give them that education.

I explain how we would go off on our own, and that upon our return we'd hose off in the yard before coming inside. I tell them that our great-grandma's home was a simple but beautiful place to be a child within, a little pot-belly stove for cooking on, an old pergola out back for sitting under. My mum – their Nan – would lounge in the front room reading; that room was always full of books.

On those trips, in the evenings, before I'd fall asleep, my own pop – their great-grandfather – would tell me he was going fishing in the morning; but that I can't come along, I am too talkative and it scares away the fish. But without fail, every morning Pop took me with him anyway. We walked down the river together, sometimes as far as the beach, and we fished as the sun rose. Sometimes the octopuses stole our bait and I always talked the whole time.

In that home on Yuin Country, when the Christmas beetles started to show up I knew my cousins would start showing up, too. We would all be there for Christmas together. I'd hide my best toys in the boot of the car so I didn't have to share and risk my older cousins accidentally breaking them.

The collective of families all found ways to cram into the house; kids sprawled on couches and mattresses in the lounge room. We lived in our swimmers and spent days rescuing Christmas beetles from spiderwebs. We kids didn't come inside until the storms or the mosquitos forced us to. When the evening storms rolled in, they brought heavy rain and the sweet heady scent of water hitting hot concrete.

I tell my kids they would have loved my Great-Grandma Lucy; she kept chickens too, and used to wear a cap that tied at the back when she watered her garden. Aunty Lisa and I loved being in the always-salty air, and took turns helping Grandma feed the chooks. She used to get all of our names mixed up, but she was kind and sometimes we walked down to the corner shop together for hot chips, carrying groceries back with us in a blue netted bag.

Time down the coast was vibrant. Mismatched tables and chairs were dragged together in the evening so the adults could play cards. They gambled using matchsticks – no kids allowed.

Before I finished primary school, my great-grandma passed away in that house. That home on Yuin Country that had a room filled with books, and an outhouse that had Aunty Lisa's feet immortalised in the slab. We wouldn't be able to holiday there anymore. But my time there is why I always hoped my own children would grow up by the water – fishing, swimming and feeding possums.

Time loops and salty air washes over us still. Now Lisa, Taylah and I are the Aunties, playing cards under my carport on Awabakal Country with Max, who is Uncle. My lounge room is home to many books and sprawled sleeping children – cousins who spend their days by the coast, fishing with grandparents, and seeking out Christmas beetles to save. Different Country: deep waterways, ancient blood, weaving together with love.

My children's attention is now lost to the television. I eat apple with them, then make sure the windows are tightly closed to keep out the smoke. There are no cousins here today. I lay on the couch and daydream about coastal Country and home Country; reflecting on the power of past, present, future, and what it means to exist within a circular understanding of time. I am grateful for my past and the future echoes I am yet to catch up to.

Casting a glance at my children, I consider that we are each and all beings with unlimited possibilities, doing our best to navigate powerful seasonal shifts. Such shifts can be forceful, magical, sometimes unpredictable, and how we prepare and respond in each season is the difference between whether we survive or whether we thrive.

ACKNOWLEDGEMENTS

ACKNOWLEDGE AND THANK MY ELDERS and family, our ancestors, descendants, community and Country, all of whom in various ways cared for me throughout the journey of firstly living these stories, and then again in writing them. I may have written this book, but it is they who collectively wrote me, and for that I am so grateful.

My parents have read and given their blessing for all that is within these pages and I want to especially thank them for allowing me to write about their eldest son, my baby brother, *Michael*, who is now with the ancestors. It was hard to write about him, but it would have been harder to have him not written in at all. My other siblings chose their own pseudonyms for their appearances in this book.

Writing and producing a book takes a team, and I am very appreciative of my publisher, Aviva, who gave me hours of time before I pitched her properly, and who throughout this process, along with the entire team at UQP, has been patient and respectful of my existence as a whole person and not just as an author.

I also acknowledge my dhagaan (brother), Odee, for his support with my ongoing relearning of our language.

Last, but not least, I wish to acknowledge Awabakal and Worimi Country, whose waterways I am immersed in on the cover of this book, and whose sky country fills my cup every evening with beautiful, restorative sunsets.

Milton Keynes UK
Ingram Content Group UK Ltd.
UKHW020635151123
432615UK00018B/879